Hidden Bhutan

Hidden Bhutan

Entering the Kingdom of
the Thunder Dragon

by
Martin Uitz

Translated by Nathaniel McBride

Armchair Traveller
at the bookHaus

First published in Germany by Picus Verlag as *Einlass ins Reich des Donnerdrachens. Verborgenes Bhutan* by Martin Utiz

This English translation first published in Great Britain in 2008 by Haus Publishing Limited

This paperback edition published in 2012 by
The Armchair Traveller *at the bookHaus*
70 Cadogan Place
London SW1X 9AH
www.thearmchairtraveller.com

A CIP catalogue record for this book is available from the British Library

ISBN 978-1-907973-16-1
ebook ISBN 978-1-907973-32-1

Typeset in Garamond by MacGuru Ltd
info@macguru.org.uk
Printed and bound by CPI Group (UK) Ltd, Croydon, CR0 4YY

Contents

Why there are No Traffic Lights in Thimphu   1
State Visit on Foot   9
The Hardest Trek in the World   18
Encounters in the Wood   26
The Hour of the Leopard   36
The Potent Caterpillar   44
Passing out in a Wooden Trough   52
The Naked Men of Bumthang   61
With a Dagger in his Belly and His Hands in Boiling Oil   70
The Visit from the Reincarnated Man   79
Electricity Comes Out of a Socket   82
Gross National Happiness   87
Outlawing Addictions   94

Glossary   100

Why there are
No Traffic Lights in Thimphu

Tales from one of the
smallest capitals in the world

He must be one of the most photographed Bhutanese in the world – the ballet dancer with the white gloves, the dapper uniform and the military helmet. The policeman who directs the traffic at Thimphu's busiest intersection from beneath a tiny pill-box is an artist. His hand movements are precisely studied and truly reminiscent of ballet. And his gaze is piercing; with it he signals to drivers with a single glance whether they should stop or go.

Thimphu must be the only capital in the world where there are no traffic lights. No one misses them, for the smartly turned-out policeman is far better suited to the city's leisurely traffic conditions than faceless electronics.

It seems that the city's planners did once want to install a set of lights at this intersection in the city centre near the main square, but they gave up when it met with resistance from the city's inhabitants. Certainly the tourists know which they prefer – during the season, dozens stand at the intersection with their cameras and capture this uniformed artist's movements on film and video.

It is hard to say how much longer this idyll is likely to last. Thimphu's volume of traffic has at least tripled over the last five years. Though traffic lights offer no competition to the likeable policeman, he's likely to have trouble with the air quality if Thimphu ever sees anything like a rush hour at nine o'clock in the morning or five o'clock in the afternoon.

The volume of traffic increases dramatically when thousands of officials and civil servants go to work or return home at the same time of day. In winter they finish work as early as four o'clock in the afternoon, in the warm summer months at five, and from one to two they have their lunch break. Bhutan's public employees take their office hours very seriously; few work overtime – which in any case is not considered a sign of particular dedication.

I had wanted to stay on at my office at the end of the working day, where I found it easier to search the Internet and concentrate on complicated work. But when I asked my official counterpart for the key to the building where we both work for the Bhutanese government, I got the following piece of advice; 'It doesn't look good if there's a light on in your room after work. People here tend to think that anyone unable to finish his work during office hours is badly organised or has something to hide.'

Thimphu remains a bureaucratic centre; the majority of those who are not self-employed work for the state administration or one of the big nationalised firms. The rhythm of life of this majority determines that of the city. Anyone working in the private sector will often be standing behind the counter or sitting at their desks twelve hours a day. For, apart from their lunch hours, these workers will know of the bureaucracy's office hours only by hearsay. Businesses stay open seven days a week, opening at nine o'clock in the morning at the latest and rarely shutting before eight at night.

By contrast, government employees are only too fond of taking the day off. On top of an impressive twenty-four national holidays, there are also religious festivals, such as the traditional *tsechus*. Then there are the occasional days off that are announced *ad hoc*, news of which spreads like wildfire. When the country's much-loved Queen Mother died, His Majesty personally decreed three days of mourning on dates determined by the astrologers. While other kinds of information can sometimes take a very long time to travel around all the government departments, news about unanticipated days off generally does the rounds with breathtaking speed.

Though the city lies 2,500 metres above sea level, snow is rare in Thimphu. One January morning, when the city lay resplendent beneath a couple of centimetres of freshly fallen snow, I decided to walk to my morning meeting at the Ministry of the Economy. On Thimphu's steep streets traffic had come to a standstill; there was no snow clearance service, no one was responsible for keeping the streets open, so I left my car and enjoyed a thirty-minute walk through the wintry city from the residential suburb of Motithang to the steep roads below the city centre. I arrived punctually outside the Ministry's main gates, only to find them closed. By way of explanation, passers-by greeted me with a 'Happy Snow Day' – didn't I know that the winter's first day of snowfall had spontaneously been declared a national holiday? Indeed, the entire city seemed to be celebrating; since early morning people had been calling each other frenziedly to pass on the news about the unexpected day off, and to make sure that no one inadvertently showed up for work.

On top of this, every Bhutanese must celebrate religious ceremonies called *pujas* several times a year. On these occasions, monks are summoned to the house, for a suitable fee, and generally spend the next three days praying for the client's health, spiritual welfare and material prosperity. Family, friends and neighbours are invited to attend these rituals. Obviously employers give individual employees days off work so they can carry out these obligations. Add to this the legally-determined four weeks' holiday a year, and Bhutan's government employees probably enjoy the highest numbers of days off in the world.

Thimphu is undoubtedly one of the smallest capitals in the world, but in recent years the Thunder Dragon's metropolis may also have become one of the fastest growing cities on earth. According to the census of 2005, almost 100,000 out of Bhutan's 634,000 inhabitants already live in the district of Thimphu, with about 70,000 of them in the city itself.

Among Bhutan's peasant population the dream of becoming rich in the city remains strong, although Thimphu could hardly be said to offer unlimited opportunities or metropolitan flair. There is a cinema, a theatre but no concert hall, a single covered sports hall, a swimming pool that has been closed for years, until recently no supermarket, no shopping malls and a very limited nightlife. Nevertheless, one gets the impression that this little city is on the verge of breaking out of its constraints, not least because of all the building that is going on in every part of it.

The city's small size allows it to recognise in advance the problems faced by other capitals in developing countries, and to solve them with foresight and planning. Thus Thimphu has no slums, an effective network of sewers, a bio-friendly sewage treatment plant set up with Danish help, good electricity and telephone services, cable TV, a modest, though relia-ble, network of state-run buses, functioning refuse collection and a system of traffic planning which makes it clear that the authorities have prepared for the city's expected growth.

Since 2006, six kilometres of motorway have linked the centre of the city with the National Highway, which connects Bhutan with India. Bhu-tan's first four-lane road has been proudly named the 'Express Highway'. It is true that the completion of the bridges has been delayed, and you still have to negotiate your way across the single-lane temporary pontoons, but that only increases the charm of the journey along the few kilometres that have already been completed. Lacking experience with the marvels of this kind of road building, Thimphu's car-owners enthusiastically drive in both directions along the new motorway, naturally on both sides of the central reservation, which is illuminated at night with colourfully flashing lights. There are no problems with drivers driving on the wrong side of the road, since oncoming traffic is present on both sides and in all directions. Even the planners' intention that people only drive on and off the Express Highway at three designated points has had to succumb to the realities of local driving habits.

There are even short-stay parking zones in Thimphu, thereby solving two problems at one stroke: for years now, more than a hundred under-qualified school leavers have been able to find jobs as parking attendants – and long-term parking in the city centre is now a thing of the past, since for every half an hour's parking the young officials charge five *ngultrum*. This can elicit startling athletic achievements on their part, for they must watch their prey with eagle eyes and sprint across to those drivers trying to sneak out of the zone without paying. 'It's a tough job, and you can never let up,' is how one young woman described the daily game of cat-and-mouse with her 'customers'.

Roughly a hundred foreigners live in Thimphu, and they either love or hate the city; no one is able to remain indifferent to the capital, which only fifty years ago consisted of barely twenty single-storey buildings.

The main complaint about life in the city is the dog problem. There are said to be more than 5,000 of these stray animals, and during the day they are to be found sleeping on pavements, quiet streetcorners and in the shade of the shutters of shopfronts. At night they live it up, fighting in barking gangs around the city limits, careering in packs after bitches on heat, howling romantically at the moon and hungrily plundering the public rubbish tips. The noise level is so high that tour operators seriously advise their clients to take ear-plugs with them for their nights in Bhutan's capital. Until 1998 the city administration fought the problem with a programme of targeted culling and sterilisation. But Thimphu's council of monks reminded it of Buddhism's basic attitude towards all living things, namely that no creature should be killed or made to suffer. There was therefore to be no decimation of dogs, who are placed fairly high in the chain of reincarnation and have a good chance of being born as humans in the next life.

Since then, no one has wanted to get their hands dirty dealing with the problem, although even the Bhutanese themselves aren't happy living in a city where gangs of dogs terrorise whole streets after nightfall. Once a female visitor, thinking I was at home, made it as far as the front door of my house, before she discovered that although the mosquito screen was open the door was locked. At her heels were a dozen yelping and snarling dogs, and she desperately took refuge between the mosquito screen and the front door – where she held out against the dogs for over two hours.

Number two on the list of complaints is the absence of bread among the goods on sale in Thimphu's grocery stores. Admittedly you can get a sweetish sliced white bread, and the 'Swiss Bakery' has made an attempt at producing something like a soft, light brown bread. But taken together it's a disaster for anyone longing for the taste of their native rye bread or pumpernickel. One place worth trying is Thimphu's only pizzeria, where some afternoons the manageress bakes a acceptable loaf of brown bread.

Bakers are a rarity among Thimphu's shopkeepers, and the best were set up by a Bhutanese who learnt his trade in Austria. Even ring-shaped *gugelhupf* and the raspberry and almond *linzertorte* are on sale as house specialities at the 'Swiss Bakery' – the creation of its original Swiss founders.

Another Austrian, Gunter Schlager, opened Thimphu's first optician's in 1992, having fallen in love here and decided to settle down.

Even harder to get hold of in Bhutan than opticians or bakers are reliable plumbers and electricians, or qualified car mechanics. It is true that Thimphu is home to the School of the Thirteen Divine Trades, but these principally serve the more honourable needs of the spirit. The School trains first-rate *thanka* painters, highly talented wood-carvers, weavers and embroiderers with a gift for traditional patterns. In their six-year courses, young artists learn painting and sculpture, how to make relief-like prayer stones and brass ornaments. But there are no training centres in Thimphu for profane necessities, such as repairing a dripping tap or changing a piston ring. As a result, getting a bathroom plumbed in or drains mended can be a nightmare, not only in the city's hotels, but also in its private houses.

Finding a carpenter isn't too difficult, but when it comes to actually making anything out of wood the inexperienced foreigner comes up against a new problem. Bhutan's woodlands are protected. Seventy per cent of the country is designated to remain forest for ever, from the subtropical rainforests in the south to the protective Alpine forests in the mountains. The felling of healthy trees is thus tightly restricted, and only the gathering of dead wood is permitted. Carpenters will accept orders, but conversations generally end with the question, 'and when will you bring me the wood?'. The astonished foreigner then learns that it is for the customer to perform the difficult task of providing raw material for the kitchen shelves or the writing desk.

But there are also expatriates who love living in Thimphu. One thing I appreciate about this funny little capital is that in the space of a few hours I can walk from my house to Phajoding, a monastic settlement 3,800 metres above sea level; from there you can gaze over the whole rapidly growing metropolis, without feeling anything of the hectic pace of the city that is slowly emerging even here. The monks of Phajoding very rarely descend to the day-to-day bustle of the town, spending years up here in meditation and contemplation.

A little way further up lies a pretty lake, at just over 4,000 metres above sea level. In the late autumn I come camping here, and found that its crystalline waters freeze at night. Up here I can meet with yakherders and their cattle, drink soup made of fermented yak cheese, try the local *eau de vie* and doze beneath the midday sun on a meadow carpeted with edelweiss and gentian.

And if I have the time, I walk up to the patch of open ground where twelve takin, Bhutan's strange national animals, lead carefree lives. It is said that the King personally ordered the takin to be taken from the small zoo and released into the wild. Keeping animals in captivity was supposedly not compatible with Buddhist principles. But the cloven-footed animals, who had got used to humans and to being regularly fed, were found determinedly trotting up and down the Norzim Lam, Thimphu's main thoroughfare, instead of running free in the wilderness. It was therefore decided that the animals be settled in a spacious open-air enclosure in a patch of wood beneath the television tower.

Is there any other city on earth where you can so easily escape the metropolitan bustle during the day and in the evening immerse yourself in small but very comfortable bars and restaurants? At the Benez, a restaurant as popular among Bhutanese as it is among *chilips* (foreigners), the illustrious visitors discuss the latest news over whisky, comparing the various news reports in the three newspapers now boasted by the country.

A beautiful new media world is steamrollering over Thimphu; television was introduced in 1999 and shortly afterwards the Internet, which is easily accessible all over the country by dialling the easy-to-remember number 100. Cable television brings over forty TV channels to virtually every household, with a selection ranging from BBC World to Indian soap operas.

For 2006 the King has finally recommended to his country that it also develop variety and competition in its print media. The newspaper *Kuensel* has been appearing since 1965, at first weekly, in English and *Dzongkha* editions, but now twice a week. The third language edition, Nepalese, was discontinued following the expulsion of the country's Nepalese minority. Since the spring of 2006 the paper, which is close to the government, has been facing competition from the *Bhutan Times*, which comes out on Sundays and has been gripping Bhutan's critical newspaper readers with its heart-warming reports and bold lay-out. The *Bhutan Observer*, published in Phuntsoling, has also been trying to carve a small corner for itself in one of the smallest newspaper markets in the world.

All this provides material for animated discussion, for the new newspapers have been testing Bhutan's press freedoms from the start. Only the figure of the King remains unassailable, enjoying not only the affection of his people but also that of journalists.

He himself lives modestly in a wooden villa up a small valley outside the city; Bhutan's 100-year-old monarchy has no royal palaces. With him live his oldest wife and the crown prince. The three younger queens – His Majesty has married four sisters – live on a magnificent estate in the upper district of Mothitang, where King Jigme Sangye regularly visits them and their children.

State Visit on Foot

Official guests weren't always welcome in Bhutan

Bhutan treats members of diplomatic missions from friendly nations with enormous politeness and attentiveness. There is scarcely a public function to which the diplomatic corps is not invited, and visits from ambassadors who do not live in Thimphu but who are accredited to Bhutan are given extended coverage in the press; diplomatic plates on their cars exempt them from having to buy road permits, and they are entitled to buy imported goods at the capital's only duty-free shop, making their lives more pleasant – in short, the kingdom has a big heart and grants a large number of privileges to the members of foreign delegations.

As a point of fact, there are, apart from the United Nations office, only two missions that hold the rank of embassies in Thimphu: one from India, the country's enormous neighbour, and one from Bangladesh, which, though it does not directly border Bhutan, is separated from the Himalayan kingdom only by a narrow corridor of land to the south. But the Bhutanese are only too pleased to accord diplomatic honours to the local offices of Western development agencies, and the Dutch and the Danish have drawn their own conclusions from this and appointed the regional chiefs of their development agencies as honorary consuls.

For decades the country's self-confident foreign policy has supported the establishment of formal diplomatic relations not only with the regional member states of the South Asian Association of Regional Co-operation (SAARC), to which Bhutan also belongs, but also with the countries of the European Union, Switzerland, the USA, Canada, Australia, Thailand, Kuwait and many others. Bhutan has been a full member of the United Nations since 1971 and plays an active role in many international and regional organisations.

All this goes on in the context of securing the kingdom's national sovereignty, which has never been in serious danger historically but whose significance has only become clear in the last third of the 20th century. The Sikkim crisis of the 1970s prompted fears in Bhutan that the country could be threatened with a similar fate. In 1975 Sikkim became, at least up to now, the last country in the Himalayas to lose its independence when it was annexed by India. By then, all the formerly independent countries of the Himalayas had become absorbed by their more powerful neighbours with the exception of Nepal and Bhutan: Tibet was occupied by China between 1950 and 1959, Kashmir was divided between India and Pakistan in the course of several wars, the formerly autonomous statelets of Ladakh and Spiti today belong to India and the independent principalities of Swat, Gilgit, Hunza and Chitral to Pakistan.

Official visitors from all over the world are received in Bhutan with every honour, diplomatic protocol is strictly observed, and Bhutan's diplomats are finally enjoying an excellent reputation internationally and have succeeded over the last few decades in nipping in the bud any doubts about their country's complete political sovereignty. Today official visitors fly to Paro in Drukair's comfortable business class, where a red carpet is rolled out for them at the airport and the guest received with great dignity in the spacious VIP lounge.

It must be said, though, that Bhutan has anything other than a historic tradition of treating the representatives and envoys of foreign powers particularly politely. Before the 1960s the country received few official foreign visitors, who tended to find the journey there arduous and, at times, their arrival decidedly unwelcome. One reason for this is that until 1964 Bhutan had no road connections with its neighbours, meaning that visitors had to go to considerable efforts to visit the country at all, even to get as far as the capital.

On the other hand, over the centuries Bhutan's rulers have had little and, at times, no desire for closer relations with foreign powers, for signing treaties or for agreeing common rules.

The first Europeans who are known to have visited Bhutan were Fathers Cacella and Cabral, Portuguese Jesuits who arrived from India in 1627 seeking a route through the country to Tibet. They reached Paro at a time when the political and religious leader *Shabdrung* Ngawang Namgyel (1593–1651) was building fortresses at strategically important points to defend the country against the Tibetans.

Though the *Shabdrung* himself showed no great interest in Christianity, he generously granted a plot of land to the two missionaries on which they could build a church. When the priests failed to find any Bhutanese willing to convert to their religion, he simply sent three of his monks to receive the sacrament. He seemed to value the presence of these foreign men of God, who evidently brought him respect among his political neighbours. But since their missionary work proved fruitless, Cacella and Cabral decided to continue with their journey and seek out the great Lama in Tibet. This proved no easy thing to do, for the *Shabdrung* simply would not let these strange visitors leave. It was only after months of negotiations that the two were finally allowed to escape his hospitality.

There are almost no reports of journeys to Bhutan from before the end of the 18th century. It was only in 1772, when the Bhutanese army occupied the Indian principality of Cooch Bihar which bordered Bhutan to the south-east, that the British colonial power began taking notice of this inaccessible mountain kingdom because of the threat it posed to peace. A punitive expedition re-established the *status quo ante*, opened negotiations that brought peace to Tibet, and led to the appointment of the British East India Company's first envoy to Bhutan in the person of George Bogle. Bogle's visit to Bhutan was much friendlier in nature and its effects are felt to this day, for the Englishman brought the first seed potatoes to the country.

However, the so-called 'Duars', a narrow strip of land directly bordering the plains of Assam and Bengal in the south-eastern foothills of the Himalayas, was to become a bone of contention between British India, its semi-autonomous principalities and the small Himalayan state. These border areas had until the 19th century largely been under Bhutanese rule; their wealth of forest and fertile and easily-farmed land were crucial to the country's economy.

The Indians and British accused the Bhutanese of occasionally kidnapping people and stealing animals and harvests from the Duars. Instead of properly administrating these rich lands, both sides were constantly trying to extort taxes and tributes from them.

These treaties and agreements set out that the Duars should sometimes be administered by the Bhutanese and at other times by the British, with each state making the appropriate tribute payments to the other in turn. Each side regularly accused the other of not making its payments on time, of embezzling funds or of not paying enough.

Although the British accounts take great pains to put the blame on the quarrelsomeness of the uncivilised and predatory Bhutanese, it is clear that behind these disputes, which went on for years, lay the colonial power's intention of annexing this area. They used the slightest pretext to impose harsh sanctions or even to threaten occupying the Duars. Every means was used to force the Bhutanese representatives to hand over British and Indian citizens who had supposedly been kidnapped, along with those responsible for the offence. By contrast, British and Indian offenders were not handed over to the Bhutanese, as the country was judged not to have a proper legal system of its own. Admittedly Bhutan had no prisons at the time; murderers had their right hands cut off and the tendons severed in their legs, which meant that there were few repeat offenders.

The British finally sent a negotiator to persuade the Bhutanese government to sign a treaty that would finally resolve the dispute over the Duars in a manner that was acceptable to the British East India Company. Ashley Eden's visit was ill-fated, and indeed the Bhutanese representatives urgently sought to have it postponed, as the situation in the country was unfavourable.

As it happened, a civil war of sorts had just broken out again in Bhutan. Its actual rulers, known by the English as the *Dharma Raja*, the country's highest-ranking and spiritual leaders, among whom were the reincarnations of the *Shabdrung* and the *Deb Raja*, had their seat of power in Punakha, but they were utterly unable to govern the country. The *Penlop* of Trongsa was fighting for supremacy with his opponents from Paro, and the princes of the kingdom were forming alternating alliances with *Dzongpens* and local tribal chiefs, while the actual government was ignored.

The British, however, only wanted to confer with the man who was supposedly the country's most important leader, and dispatched Eden to negotiate with him. On his way there, Eden repeatedly ignored all advice to turn back, as the government in Punakha was not ready for his visit.

He set out in winter, crossing snow-bound passes in appalling weather conditions. It is not clear whether the Bhutanese deliberately sent him by circuitous and barely accessible routes, but it is certainly the case that the Englishman chose one of the most difficult ways into the country, from Darjeeling directly into the Ha Valley, instead of following the considerably better route through Sikkim and the Chumbi Valley in Tibet.

Eden was deserted by most of his bearers, and the stubborn envoy was forced to leave behind the majority of his baggage and supplies. As he travelled, local princes repeatedly tried to persuade him to turn back, but Eden would not do so without a written declaration from the government in Punakha that his visit was unwelcome.

Eden was hardly the best of choices for this difficult mission. His opinion of the Bhutanese becomes clear from reading his reports, in which the government of Bhutan comes across as a pack of greedy, intransigent and unscrupulous political rivals, who are constantly fighting each other for a place in the sun. Eden himself is revealed as being hardly free from prejudices. The uninvited guest claims to have been treated by the country's authorities 'with a loutish lack of decorum and a shocking callousness'.

As it was, he made his way to Punakha despite all these warnings, where the Bhutanese gave him a reception that at the very best could hardly be said to correspond to normal diplomatic protocol. The Trongsa *Penlop*, who effectively led the negotiations, wanted to force Eden to sign a treaty that would provide for the complete return of the Duars, which had been occupied by the British, together with the payment of large reparations. When Eden refused to sign this, the *Penlop* personally rubbed wet earth into his face, pulled his hair and hit him on the back – much to the amusement of his assembled officials. The *Dzongpen* of Wangdue Phoedrang wanted to make his own contribution to the proceedings, and urged Dr Simpson, the expedition's surgeon, to swallow some *doma* (acrea nut with betel leaves) that he had chewed himself. When the latter refused, the *Penlop* spat the red pulp in his face.

Eden signed the humiliating treaty, while noting beneath his signature, 'under compulsion'; in return he was accorded safe passage out of the kingdom. He now took to his heels, and marching day and night reached Paro in two days; in another ten, he was in Darjeeling.

For the British, the humiliation of their envoy was now a *causus belli*. Despite several attempts by the Bhutanese government to keep negotiations going, British and Indian troops occupied the much-coveted Duars, imagining they had successfully implemented a policy that had taken little regard for the rights and interests of their small neighbour to the north.

They were therefore appalled when the Bhutanese launched a devastating counter-attack in January 1865. 'Our losses could not have been greater if the enemy had had firearms,' is how a British officer described the terrible effect of the Bhutanese arrows, which were launched with great accuracy from traditional bamboo bows.

The colonial power's fleeing troops left behind two howitzers, dozens of wounded men, the greater part of their munitions and supplies for twelve days, after the Trongsa *Penlop* successfully attacked the border town of Dewangiri (today Samdrup Jongkhar) with only 1,200 men.

It wasn't until March that the British and their Indian troops succeeded in forcing the Bhutanese back to the edge of the mountains. Plans were now being laid for an invasion of Bhutan, which was to begin after the rainy season. These were never realised, for Bhutanese negotiators signalled themselves ready to sue for peace. The British government's basic demands were met: a public apology for the treatment given to Ashley Eden, the return of the two captured howitzers and acceptance of British occupation of the Duars in return for an annual payment.

After cutting down the valuable tropical forest, the British colonial power transformed the Duars into gigantic tea plantations. Many thousands of migrant workers were settled there, most of them from Nepal, who have since then given the region a very different character.

Yet there were official visitors who, unlike Ashley Eden, sang the praises of Bhutanese hospitality, courtesy and kindness. In 1905 Jean-Claude White had the honour of conferring upon 'his friend Ugyen Wangchuk' – as he himself described him – the order and title of Knight Commander of the Indian Empire. This high honour, which carried the title of 'Sir', was awarded to the man who would later become the first King of Bhutan in recognition of his services as a member of the British delegation to Tibet.

Two years later, White, as an honoured guest and envoy of the British throne, was involved in selecting and appointing Trongsa *Penlop* to the rank of first *Druk Gyalpo*; that is, king of a finally unified Bhutan. He missed no opportunity to describe his journeys to Bhutan as being among the most memorable high points of his life, showing great affection for his Bhutanese friends and taking considerable pains to correct Eden's harsh comments on the country.

White ascribed to mere prejudice Eden's description of the Bhutanese as particularly dirty and ill-mannered, a people who never let water near their bodies unless it was for the purposes of distilling liquor. He wrote that 'my experience with the people was that they were generally polite, civilised and clean. During my entire stay I saw only one man who was drunk'. We may assume this was something of an understatement.

The last important statesman to pay a visit to Bhutan on foot was the Indian prime minister Jawaharlal Nehru. In 1958 he was planning on visiting Tibet, but the country on the roof of the world was then on the verge of the great Khampa uprising against its Chinese occupiers. So Nehru changed his travelling plans, crossing on foot the 4,500-metre high Nathu-La on the border between Sikkim and Tibet, and descending into Tibet's Chumbi Valley, where he turned sharply east.

For centuries this had been the shortest route into western Bhutan, leading to Paro and Punakha, then the capital of the country. Nehru rode and walked for five days as far as Paro, accompanied by, among others, his then forty-year-old daughter Indira.

'Somehow, the Himalayas convey not only a spirit of peace, but also of permanence beyond human follies', is how his biographer describes Nehru's thoughts. The powerful politician is said to have felt 'carefree' as he found himself temporarily liberated from his everyday concerns.

To this day, Bhutanese ascribe the remarkable content of his conversations with the Third King, Jigme Dorji Wangchuk, to his encounter with their culture, which greatly impressed Nehru during his travels in the Land of the Thunder Dragon. He had not come, he said, as the representative of a powerful nation that aimed to put pressure on its small neighbour. Bhutan should remain an independent country for ever, following its own way and determining its own pace of progress.

The treaty between India and Bhutan of 1949 had clearly provided a leading role for India in deciding matters of international policy, while Bhutan would only remain in full control of its internal affairs. Following Nehru's visit this basic position changed, and the Indian government supported Bhutan's application to join the Colombo Plan. In 1964 Bhutan gained – also with India's support – full membership of the international postal union, becoming for the first time an equal member in a global organisation. Stamp collectors all over the world were among the first foreigners properly to notice the existence of the small Himalayan kingdom: for years Bhutan has produced vast quantities of stamps using the most unusual techniques – to the despair of many collectors.

India sent experts to Bhutan, who at the beginning of the 1960s helped their small neighbour develop its first five-year plan. India also financed most of the costs of this development policy. Following the closing of the border with Tibet and the catastrophe of the Indo-Chinese Himalayan war, the road was built from the Indian border through Phuntsholing to Thimphu and Paro. The country is now connected with the Indian sub-continent's road network by 170 kilometres of mountain roads, varying in their height above sea level by almost 3,000 metres, and winding countless turns through the most difficult terrain.

Since then, heads of state have no longer had to come on foot when paying an official visit to the country.

The Hardest Trek in the World

Reasons for taking the Snowman Trek during the monsoon

'You will not see any mountains!' said the Japanese tourist with an undertone of conviction. He told us that he'd only come because it was the season for blue poppies. It was 14 July, and a damp, cold evening above the meadows of Jangothang. Jomolhari and Jichu Drake were hidden somewhere in the clouds. The Japanese looked pleased to be on his way back down; a little further uphill, at Lake Tsophu, he had come across the blue and purple blooms of hundreds of phosphorescent anemones.

The next day, 15 July, was my wife's birthday. We woke at six, and shortly afterwards the monsoon clouds lifted for about twenty minutes, giving us a marvellously clear view of what is perhaps one of Bhutan's most beautiful mountain peaks. It immediately put us in a good mood; marvelling at it, we could not help smiling. The mountain is the domain of the gods, and in July their throne is whiter than if it were covered with ermine. On its summit, between 7,000 and 7,500 metres above sea level, the monsoon falls as snow, making the Jomolhari shine all the more brilliantly in the morning sun.

For the next three weeks, the Japanese man would remain the only tourist we came across. But neither would we see any more mountains.

Anyone planning on going trekking just once in their lives in the Himalayas should avoid the monsoon season. The danger of returning drenched and disappointed is just too great. But those who have been bitten by the trekking bug, those who keep coming back, planning, every year, an ever more daring route, those who enjoy the fourth week of trekking more than the first – they should try it: trekking during the monsoon is one of the last real challenges the Himalayas offer to a fairly small group of (admittedly) rather odd people.

But why take the Snowman Trek, which, according to *Lonely Planet*, is 'one of the most difficult treks in the world', involving twenty-five days' of walking over no less than twelve passes, none lower than 4,500 metres?

There are good reasons. You have to hold out some hope that it won't rain incessantly. And you need a small measure of optimism and even *joie de vivre*, since for every drop of rain, a flower blooms on the high mountain pastures: edelweiss in such quantities that you could mow it with a scythe, primrose and mountain daisy, anemones and foxgloves – and of course the blue poppies, Bhutan's national flower, indigenous only to regions above 4,000 metres.

The veil of fog and the warm summer temperatures bring animals to up the high mountain pastures, who normally would be hiding deep in impenetrable forest. You are more likely to see (and see more clearly) bears, blue sheep and the extremely rare takin during the monsoon season, since above the treeline there are fewer places for them to hide. In the summer they are followed by timid hunters such as the snow leopard, which can be found in regions far above 5,000 metres.

There is an abundance of mushrooms. Even at 5,000 metres, night temperatures barely fall below freezing. This means that in summer you will avoid one of the Snowman Trek's greatest risks, that of being trapped between passes by fresh falls of snow.

There are also, it must be said, leeches. For many this is the main reason to avoid trekking during the monsoon. But, as you may have guessed, you won't come across them on the Snowman Trek. Its route covers heights of between 3,700 and 5,400 metres, which is too high even for leeches.

The summer offers another reward in the pastures of Robluthang. The rare takin spends the warm, damp summer in an remote and idyllic valley, drawn by a salty marsh on the bank of a small river. Takin are among the strangest large mammals in the world. It is believed that there are only a few hundred of them left in the wild. We saw about a hundred of them during the monsoon month of July, after our packhorses had taken a different route across the valley so that they would not disturb the timid creatures. Although the horses passed them at a great distance, the takin fled deeper into the woods for a while.

It was here, many miles from human settlement, that we encountered a friendly ranger. He was a member of the Royal Guards, charged with protecting these strange animals. He advised us to wait for a while, find a place to hide behind some rocks and to make as little noise as possible. The takin would come back. About an hour later, they duly did; first the older and stronger animals, followed by the young with their mothers. They trotted slowly back to the salty ground by the banks of the river, relaxed and perhaps a little antediluvian in their movements. Though a protected species in Bhutan for over three decades now, they still haven't yet got used to the fact that they are no longer being hunted.

According to legend, Drukpa Kinley, the 'divine madman' is said to have created these strange creatures. Following a sumptuous banquet given him by poor shepherds, the holy man supposedly assembled the remaining bones of a cow they had eaten, setting upon its neck the head of a goat. The result was the takin (*Budocras Taxicolor*), today Bhutan's 'national animal'.

Even in good weather, the trek across the 5,005-metre high Sinche La is extremely demanding. On this particular day the monsoon showed us what it was capable of. It was raining when we struck the tents in the morning, and the rain continued to beat down during the five-hour climb up to the pass, whose monotony was broken only by wild dogs belonging to the yakherders who were camping nearby. In good weather they'd probably have kept these yelping animals tied up, but who was likely to be passing by in such appalling conditions? It was raining and bitterly cold when we got to the top of the pass, and it rained as we descended, until we arrived at tent woven from yak hair where a friendly herdswoman plied us with *suja* (butter tea). However, on that day even the tent, the product of eighteen months' manual labour, could barely withstand the rain, and leaked in dozens of places. Then it rained the rest of the way down to Limithang.

All this time my sons Fabian and Lukas, then fifteen and sixteen years old, and I were completely unaware of the fact that we were soaked through, but went on chatting and letting our thoughts wander. We lost contact with Renee, Sophie and David, who wanted to reach the camping site as fast as possible with the pack horses. It is only later that we noticed that the little stream we were following was literally growing stronger with every minute that passed. Further down we saw Renee and the others; they had already managed to reach the other bank, but for us it was too late. Wading across was out of the question now; the steady rain had turned the harmless stream into a torrential river, that seemed to grow ever more threatening by the minute. On the other side of the river our helpers started building an emergency bridge out of tree trunks. It was a race against time, for the churning stream of water was relentlessly spreading its banks, throwing up rocks and boulders around itself, thundering around us with a deafening noise and thwarting our attempts to bridge it. The slippery trunks were wedged between rocks, and, with trembling knees, we clambered precariously across them to the other bank, where helpful hands received us.

By now the spot where we'd pitched our tents was under 10 centimetres of water, and the blue plastic sheeting that covered them was dripping and leaking in every place.

I woke during the night. It had suddenly become very quiet, and the noise of the rushing stream had almost completely subsided. Stars glittered in the sky, and behind the tent the snowy fields of the Great Tiger Mountain were shining in the moonlight. Soon the morning sun transformed the raindrops still hanging from the primroses and rhododendrons into silver pearls.

That's how quickly things can change during the monsoon.

There are very few villages along this remarkable trek. Chebisa is one such settlement, charmingly situated in a gentle green valley into which flows a picturesque waterfall. Around it are mountain pastures and snow-capped peaks. We saw great herds of blue sheep on the ridges above the village, while above us bearded vultures circled majestically. Two hawks sliced through the thin air; the place was like something out of a picture book. We pitched our little tents and bathed in a nearby stream, icy cold with glacier water. It was a pure idyll.

The village was empty, with not a soul in sight. The doors of the sturdy stone houses were bolted shut, and no one was home. In summer Bhutan's mountain dwellers move up to the high mountain pastures with their yaks, often several days' walk from their villages. There they live as nomads, moving to new pasture grounds every three or four weeks, and only returning to their winter settlements in the late autumn.

It was already dark and we had settled comfortably in our tents when Lukas had to go out again to pee. He searched around for some bushes near our campsite with a flashlight. A few minutes later he came back. 'There's a dog sitting behind the bushes. I saw his eyes quite clearly by the light of the torch.' It only occurred to me a little while later that there could be no dogs left in the village; they would naturally have followed the owners up to the pastures. So whose eyes had Lukas seen in the bushes? Just then we saw a dark shadow move as the animal ambled away.

Our team were very excited, for the black Himalayan bear is the most feared of animals among the Bhutanese. Though apparently good-natured, the creature is actually moody and unpredictable, and frequently seeks confrontations with human beings. It is best given a wide berth. A few days later we came across another one, this time in full daylight, peacefully feeding amid some bushes that overhung the opposite bank of the river. Nevertheless, our local companions immediately took to their heels.

The journey from the charming village of Laya to far-flung Thansa in the Lunana mountains passes through one of the most remarkable and beautiful stretches of country that can be found in the Himalayas. It was particularly unforgettable for us, for during this time the monsoon lifted for an entire week. There were five days of cloudless skies, summer temperatures and the most beautiful views of Mount Luana, 7,000 metres high and covered in snow. Such things are possible even during the 'rainy season'.

I spent our rest day in Laya explaining to the village head and the caravan leader that, from the next day on, we would only need nine pack animals. Only my two younger sons wanted to attempt the Snowman Trek's royal leg; Renee, Sophie and David would descend to the warm springs at Gasa. Two weeks of high passes and monsoon had been enough for them.

After a great deal of palaver, the pack animal handler eventually agreed to reduce the number of yaks we'd ordered to nine, on condition that we paid cash in advance – although not before he'd foisted on us, at a vastly inflated price, a caravan of horses for my wife's journey down the mountain.

From the military camps below Layam a long climb leads up to the high mountain pastures at Rodophu, and it was here that the nine yaks were to relieve our horses the next day. When we arrived we were astonished to find sixteen yaks herded together. The yakherder spoke no English, and only shrugged his shoulders in answer to my questions, indicating that we should go on ahead and leave him and his nephews to load the baggage themselves. In preparation we had carefully divided our belongings among eighteen packs, to be loaded onto nine yaks.

The sixteen yaks caught up with us at midday; all seemed to be fully loaded, with their burdens stuffed into potato sacks so it was impossible to tell what the shaggy cattle animals were actually carrying. The yakherder's expression was inscrutable.

That evening we were surprised to come across the yak owner, who initially had not shown the least interest in coming with us. He explained his change of heart, and the extra packs, quite simply: he was bringing 'merchandise for the people in Thansa, who get very few traders'. The goods came from China and Tibet, and a messenger was sent on ahead to announce that a market was coming to Thansa.

The remote villages on Bhutan's north-western border with Tibet derive a good deal of their 'merchandise' from their neighbour, who can be reached in a day's march over 5,000-metre high passes. Legally this is smuggling, though the trade is commonplace and has been going on for centuries. Tibetans also cross the passes into Bhutan, generally to gather herbs illegally, including the cordyceps fungus. In this way Chinese goods find their way into Bhutan's mountain villages.

So far, the arrival of *chilips* (foreigners) has had relatively little effect on the people of Thansa. Far more important to them are the colourful rubber boots, thermos flasks and fleece jackets that the caravan leader unloaded from his mysterious extra pack animals. The bargaining and haggling went on for hours. With the onset of evening, our yak driver disappeared together with a couple of important-looking local men, only to return hours later looking pleased with themselves and with an impressive amount of *chyang* (a slightly alcoholic drink brewed from wheat or millet). Not only did they have their successful sale of their 'merchandise' to celebrate, but had also, as they frankly told me, sold 'for a good price' the yak whose ill-temper had caused them so many problems on the journey up.

The route over the Luanan mountains from Thansa to the hot springs at Duer Tsachu has been described as the hardest test along the Snowman Trek. You have to camp four times above 5,000 metres; but three weeks in the mountains is generally enough time to acclimatise to this, and you should be able to fully enjoy the remarkable experience of these days and nights. Every day the monsoon sent clouds and rain against us, but whenever we came across some especially beautiful mountain, glacier, alpine lake or rockface it would mercifully lift its cloudbanks and give us glimpses of views that would stay with us for a long time to come. We walked for hours over meadows of edelweiss, saw blue poppies, which tend to grow in the rocky interzone between meadow and alpine heath, and delighted in the chanterelles that grow right next to the path in this remote area.

After dark it grew very quiet; above 5,000 metres, the gurgling brooks and small lakes freeze solid for a couple of hours at night. This means it is better to attempt difficult river crossings in the early morning, since the streams carry less water at that time of day. The real danger is not so much the strength of the current but the coldness of the water, which after only a few minutes drives all sensation from toes and feet. Since you can't feel the tops of the stones on the river bed, it is easy to hurt yourself or stumble and fall victim to the unpredictable glacier stream. For this reason we always crossed the rivers together, with each of us watching carefully where the other treads, and, if needed, ready to extend a helping hand.

'Dad, can we stay here another day?' When a fifteen-year-old asks his father this kind of a question after twenty days of walking, then it says a great deal about the quality of a place that, a few days before they reach the end of it, rewards all trekkers on the Snowman for their hardship and effort. Duer Tsachu (the hot springs of Duer) lies hidden in a valley on one side of the river Mangdi. Guru Rimpoche meditated here 1,300 years ago, and anyone coming here today and making the effort to feel the spirit of the place will also lapse into humility and meditation.

From the rocks of a narrow valley a dozen hot springs burst forth; some naturally carbonated and bubbling, others so hot you have to add cold water to take a bath in them. Known for centuries for their healing properties, simple bathing places of stone and wood have been built right next to the springs, just big enough for one or two people to enjoy the refreshment of a thermal bath together.

Few visitors find their way to Duer Taschu. The passes to the east and west of the springs are too high and too strenuous for most, limiting access to them to the months between June and September.

The last two passes on the way to Bumthang are not listed in the few trekking guides that contain any information on the Snowman Trek. They bring the number to a round dozen. Over the last few days the monsoon rains had reduced the path in certain places to a swamp-like morass. We constantly found ourselves getting stuck, losing our shoes and sinking up to our thighs in the mud. But through all this we remained cheerful. The fourth week of trekking in the monsoon is more beautiful and carefree than the first.

Encounters in the Wood

*There are places where even
a queen has to travel on foot*

Sure, the road from Tashitang to Damji was now passable; perhaps a little slippery after the rain, but no problem for a four-wheel-drive vehicle. This reassuring piece of advice, provided us by the *mangap* or village headman, proved in practice to be a classic case of glossing things over. The first 15 kilometres of the route were covered with stones that stuck vertically out of the earth, while the remaining 10 were an incredibly slippery trek through mud and swamp that bore virtually no resemblance to a road.

I stopped many times and went ahead on foot to check whether the road ahead of us was passable at all. With my foot right down on the gas, the Toyota Prado wallowed through the muddy soup. As night began to fall we finally reached the small village of Damji, where the *mangap* was already waiting for us.

To our surprise he had found a horseman who could speak some broken English; Namgay immediately brought us down to his house, where he lived with his rather brusque young wife, her parents and four sisters. We were offered red rice, chilli and salt tea – food to keep us going on the strenuous route from Gasa to Laya.

At 4,400 square kilometres, Gasa is both Bhutan's largest and least-populated province; altogether only 3,300 people live in its villages, most of which lie in high mountain regions. Gasa is the only remaining provincial capital that cannot be reached by road; to get a view of it, you have to march for six hours over rope bridges spanning deep crevasses and past picturesque waterfalls. Below it, at Mo Chhu, is the *Tsachu*, the hot springs of Gasa, famed throughout Bhutan for their healing properties. Five hundred metres further up and clinging precipitously to the side of a mountain is the impressive *Dzong*, formerly a fortress built by the *Shabdrung* to secure the nearby border with Tibet, and today a monastery and seat of the provincial government.

The second day's march leads over the Beri-La, 3,900 metres high, into a side valley of the Mo Chhu, where, according to *Lonely Planet*, there is to be found the most uncomfortable camping site in the whole of the Himalayas. For that reason we wanted to travel further, if possible to the Army Camp, two hours' march below Laya. But the climb through almost endless forest was difficult; above 1,300 metres, the way is hampered by tree roots and large stones, as well as swamps and hundreds of large and small streams. Nevertheless I felt great; the giant trees around me felt like friends, willing to tell me of the many centuries they had lived. One could only imagine who they had seen come by this way. Further up, coyote lichen hung like beards from the wooden giants. The pair of vultures we met along the way did not disturb us; for them the season was already over.

For my companion, however, the strenuous march was simply too much. Despite all the trekking experience she had gained in Nepal, the routes in Bhutan seemed to be of a different order: far steeper and more exhausting, so that often you had to sit down at every step if you didn't want to topple over or fall. I found myself having to wait for her a lot. By the time we got to the top of the pass, it was clear we weren't going to make it to the Army Camp the same day. But our horses, together with our thermoses, sleeping bags and dry clothes were already ahead of us, unaware that we couldn't keep up with them. I arrived in Konia at about two o'clock in the afternoon. Amid the marshy terrain stood a single stone-built house, looked after by a lonely old man whose thick glasses concealed a pair of inflamed eyes. Ulla arrived, exhausted, a little before four o'clock.

We then had to make a quick decision, for while I had been waiting my chances of making it to the Army Camp while it was still daylight had sunk to virtually nil. Ulla was to stay here, where the old man would offer her shelter and cook her some soup. I had to catch up with the caravan and be in Laya the next day. Ulla lent me her flashlight, since I would be travelling with virtually no equipment. From here the route headed up the valley of Mo Chhu, crossing two smaller passes. By about six o'clock it would be dark in Bhutan, added to which there was a new moon.

In the twilight, I descended from the second pass along a steep track, back into the gully of the torrential river, and it was there that I heard something moving in a bamboo thicket growing along the steep slope to the left of the path. I had been warned that, only the day before yesterday, a bear had killed four pigs in Gasa.

The cracking sound continued; then I clearly saw the bamboo branches move: a pair of round brown hindquarters shone ahead of me. Takin! Their thick, muscular bodies make the shy animals appear clumsy, though they can climb the steepest rock faces as nimbly as mountain goats. These two magnificent specimens fled from me through the mountain forest.

Over the river below me I saw a cantilevered bridge, of the kind that for centuries have spanned Bhutan's most difficult terrain and most torrential mountain streams. Untroubled by the fact it was nearly dark, I jogged round the edge of a cliff – and found another takin standing right in the middle of the path to the bridge. This time it was a young one, six months old and as big as a calf.

The young animal looked at me guilelessly; I saw that his pelt was lighter than that of full-grown animals, with two parallel light brown stripes running lengthways from his thick neck to his hindquarters. I too stood still. Were I to have stretched out my hand then, I could actually have touched the strange animal. How long did we gaze at each other? It might have been a minute, perhaps two. Then I took a step forward and the takin made a sudden leap back as far as the bank of the river, where he suddenly stood still again.

On the bank opposite, my horse driver's wife had been watching our strange meeting. Both of them had stopped here; an inner voice must have whispered to them that I was too far behind to have been able to make it all the way to the Army Camp before nightfall.

Namgay had discovered a rocky overhang beneath which we would be able to spend a dry night. We cooked first *suja* and then rice on the camp fire. A piece of branch served as our cooking spoon, and the couple divided their plates of rice with me, while Namgay cut the top off a discarded plastic bottle to serve as a teacup. Needless to say, I had left my modest supply of cutlery in Ulla's rucksack.

We laid blankets round the edge of the rock and stowed our pack where it was dry, then gave nosebags to our horses and the donkey in recompense for the long day's walk. I like sleeping outside at the worst of times, but I liked it all the more in this unspoilt spot where shepherds had probably been camping for centuries.

After it got dark it started raining again. But it was dry where we were lying beneath the rock. I was soon asleep, and all night was visited by the most marvellous dreams. My assumption that the water and raindrops would follow the laws of gravity and fall straight to the earth from the outer edge of the rock proved false: in the darkness, tiny streams of water clung to the rock, crossed the edge and ran, apparently counter to all the laws of nature, diagonally inwards across the ceiling of rock until, confronted with a quietly sleeping *chilips* beneath them, fell directly onto my sleeping bag. But who can be bothered by such details on such a magnificent night?

It was another hour and a half's walk to the Army Camp. I was supposed to present my papers there, but when we arrived no one seemed to pay the least bit of attention to me. On the far bank of a stream, a colourfully decked-out reception committee of Bhutanese and Indian officers was waiting on a helipad amid the sacred fumes of burning juniper branches and rhododendron leaves. They were evidently expecting a visit by someone very important.

A young officer invited me to join his delegation in attending the imminent arrival of *Ashi* Sangay Choden. For the last two weeks, the youngest of Bhutan's four queens had been travelling from Paro to Laya by way of Lingshi, as part of her work as a UNESCO ambassador providing education on family planning, hygiene, women's rights and HIV/AIDS prevention.

A few minutes later a small but determined-looking woman appeared. She was in her early forties and wore a broad-brimmed hat, tied about with a cloth of the royal yellow-gold, together with a half-*kira* made of the finest silk, a variation of the traditional Bhutanese full-body wrap-around skirt for women which covered only her hips and legs. Behind her a whole phalanx of people pushed and shoved; bodyguards, permanent secretaries, high officials, officers in the uniform of the Guard, mayors, flunkeys, favourites and people who were hoping to become favourites.

The young commander barked his report, which Her Highness received calmly, then crossed the road and turned to me. I noticed that the surface of her fair-skinned face shone slightly; was it a trace of royal sweat, or the remains of a moisturising cream? 'How are you this morning?' Her English did not betray the slightest accent. 'Are you here all alone?'

I tell her that I'm on my way to meet some friends in Laya. 'Tough guys, they want to go all the way to Bumthang'; the *Ashi* was well informed: she had met the six of them only the evening before. I tell her of my meeting with the takin, and the night under the rock. A smile passed across her face that expressed both earnestness and a trace of melancholy. Was I fooling myself, or was she actually enjoying the fact that an uncouth foreigner was recounting stories to her without his eyes lowered, or in a whisper, or with his right hand humbly held in front of his mouth. After a quarter of an hour she wished me a good journey. 'Safe journey, Your Highness!' I blurted out, only to learn my *faux pas* an hour later – it should have been 'Your Majesty'.

As I headed further on towards Laya I found my way continuously hampered by the royal train: about seventy pack horses and mules, led by dozens of soldiers and caravan drivers, were carrying tons of baggage. Along with provisions and tents, gas cylinders and cooking utensils, what struck me most were the two diesel generators that produced electricity for the loudspeakers they had brought with them. The *Ashi* held large meetings with the inhabitants of the mountain villages, and marquees with lots of coloured flags, folding chairs and even a sound system were set up in playing fields and schoolyards. She warns people about the dangers of AIDS, a central theme of her campaign.

One might think that AIDS itself is not a great problem in Bhutan. There are fewer than eighty recorded cases of HIV infection, and until now only a few deaths. People with the disease are limited to the urban centres of Phuntsholing and Thimphu, and almost all those infected have either caught the virus directly from visiting a brothel in the Indian border province of Jaigaon, or indirectly from their husbands. The Bhutanese, however, are able planners, and wise enough to enjoy anticipating the future: a single case of AIDS in one of the remote mountain valleys such as Laya or Lingshi could easily lead to a catastrophe. For in these extremely thinly populated areas with their comparatively liberal sexual traditions, an entire valley could quickly become infected. Laya has only 800 inhabitants, but traditions of polygamy and polyandry mean that the sexual encounters among them are far more numerous than one would expect among such a comparatively small population. As a result, educational work goes on in regions where until now there has not been a single infection.

Following the *Ashi's* speech, music with melancholy lyrics is played, illustrating and highlighting what the audience has just heard through popular tunes. Health officials then explain very clearly how to use condoms, and samples are generously handed out. Most of them, however, won't be used for their proper purpose: the village children find it fascinating to blow them up like balloons – or so, at least, their ubiquity might lead one to imagine.

Bhutan's health policy is uncompromising. The kingdom does everything it can to recognise dangers posed by new diseases and prevent them entering its territory. During the SARS epidemic a few years ago, the tiny country took drastic measures when for a short time its borders were closed to those travelling from affected areas. Tourists who had paid the official minimum tariff of $200 a day on top of an expensive flight arrived at the airport at Paro to be unceremoniously offered the choice of spending several weeks quarantined in the local hospital or flying back home the next day. Since the outbreak of bird flu, importing birds or eggs to Bhutan has been strictly forbidden, leading to a dramatic fall in the supply of eggs in Thimphu.

At over 3,900 metres above sea level, Laya is one of the highest settlements in Bhutan that is inhabited all year round. And it is also the most beautiful of mountain villages in the Bhutanese Himalayas, situated on a gently sloping pasture at the foot of several mountains that are over 7,000 metres high and covered by an eternal snow, among them the Great Tiger Mountain. The Layaps are a people with their own language and traditions, and visitors are fond of photographing the women, whose hats are woven out of bamboo and crowned by a stick that looks like a lightning rod.

Apart from photographers, the Layaps have little contact with Bhutan and its government. It is only eight hours from here to the Tibetan border, where that consumer giant, China, offers riches to delight a Bhutanese heart: rubber boots, fleece jackets, thermos flasks, carpets, transistor radios or solar panels which farmers mount on the wooden slat roofs of their traditionally-built houses. All these goods should never have crossed the country's closed borders. For until now Bhutan and China have maintained no diplomatic relations, and – at least officially – no direct trade over the Himalayan passes.

But the altruistic Layaps have other ideas, and have dedicated themselves to the service of a good cause by providing transport for these goods – over secret routes and smugglers' paths that only they know. It also seems likely that in return they sell to Tibet and China cordyceps, a fungus with supposedly miraculous properties. Harvesting the powerful mushrooms has occasionally brought them into conflict with Tibetans who make their way over the border in early summer to go looking for it themselves. The fungus has been prized for centuries by Chinese medicine for its curative properties.

I was short of time on the way back, and consequently wanted to make the descent from Laya to Gasa in one day. The horse driver quickly agreed; the route from Damji to Laya is still calculated at three days' rental of the horses, irrespective of how quickly the client travels. The horses remained behind; we had agreed to walk as far as Gasa without taking a midday rest, and hopefully to get there before darkness fell. It was a distance of almost 40 kilometres, more than 2,000 metres uphill and 3,000 down.

As we were climbing up to Beri-La it started to drizzle.

Even up here at 3,300 metres, the forest to the right and left of us was very dense. Suddenly we heard cracking in the undergrowth. A bear appeared, looking hesitant and good-natured. After a few seconds he turned around and disappeared growling into the thicket.

The encounter was so sudden and over so quickly that I had no time to be afraid.

One hundred and fifty metres further on I saw on the left some resting places laid out with brushwood and juniper, which had been placed there at regular intervals by the delegation's advance guard for the use of the *Ashi*, who must have come this way the same morning. Now, though, there were two tents standing there, and a little further uphill the cooking tent of the team accompanying a tourist group that had pitched its camp in the middle of the forest.

It was an inhospitable place to be camping, in the rain alongside the track. The three tourists had closed their tents and were probably waiting inside until the rain was over. Their guide invited me into the cooking tent and offered me tea and cakes.

In a hushed voice I told him of my meeting with the bear, scarcely a stone's throw from where his group was camping. I could see that this piece of news did not please him. In such cases there's only one thing you can do: make a lot of noise, for bears hate commotion. So they started hammering pots and singing. The clients were not informed; they had enough to worry about with the rigours of the weather.

Fortified by the tea, I continued on, crossing the pass and then sliding over ever muddier paths down the 1,400 metres to Gasa. At six it was already pitch dark in the dense primeval forest. Half an hour later, I knocked on the wooden shed of a shop in Gasa's market place, where we had spent the night three days before.

The next morning was devoted to bathing in the hot springs below Gasa, on the banks of the Mo Chhu. About a hundred pack horses blocking the entrance bore witness to the presence of royalty. Hosts of vultures plagued them, drawn by the warm scent of blood from their muzzles and nostrils. *Ashi* Sangay Choden had invited the local women's group to a talk.

The several pools about the hot springs are covered over by pavilions, each of which offers space for fifteen to twenty bathers. A large pool in the middle of the area serves as a horse-bath. The royal horsemen were going to great and subtle lengths to lure the royal stud farm's magnificent steeds into the water. It was no easy task, for the kingdom's proudest horses are somewhat afraid of water.

Bhutan has a great tradition of hot baths. Dozens of *tsachus* are to be found in the eastern Himalayas. Even Guru Rimpoche meditated in these holy places, and the springs' healing properties have been known for centuries. Gasa is the largest of all the baths, and its reputation today of being dirty and overcrowded is not in the least justified. The *Ashi*'s visit had been taken as a pretext for everyone to go bathing.

Bathing is mixed. Signs request that visitors be properly dressed, but when I was there neither men nor women had on more than a towel around their hips or a pair of underpants. The young nun in the middle pavilion was a little more conscious of her modesty and covered both her breasts and her hips with red towels; but the elderly farmer's wives are more robust and quite unashamed to show that the breasts and bottoms of older Bhutanese ladies are remarkably firm.

People gossip at the baths. This is a favourite pastime in a country where sensational events are rare and where one can consequently make oneself popular by being the bearer of news. There are no differences in dress here to discourage people talking to each other; since everyone is naked, no one can tell anyone else's social standing, and hierarchies, otherwise so powerful, are forgotten. A cameraman from BBS (Bhutan Broadcasting Services) told us all about his days spent travelling with the *Ashi*, whom he accompanied on her journey to the remote villages. A series of runners take the tapes they record to Thimphu, so they are able to provide half-way up-to-date reports from the mountain regions, which are still not yet connected to telephone or electricity networks.

Now that Gasa has recently been connected to the electricity grid, television will also be arriving here and will probably at least in part put an end to the practice of pleasant story-telling, and the informal spreading of rumours and news among bathers at the *Tsachu*.

The Hour of the Leopard

*Why six men should never try
doing anything together*

The Dagala Trek is also known as the Thousand Lake Trek – something of an overstatement, given that the high-lying valleys around Dagala have about twenty-five larger and fifty smaller bodies of water. It is recommended that tourists make the tour in early summer; walking this route during the monsoon season requires just a touch of foolhardiness, along with a certain minimum of high spirits and waterproofing. My son Fabian and I were longing for the high mountain pastures, my friend Tshering and his cousin Sangay were willing to come along, and Sonam, our guide, together with Dava, our cook, completed the team. Pack horses were ordered and baskets with provisions and cooking equipment were packed. We were to leave the next day.

That evening the telephone rang. A few hours before we were about to set off, Tshering ruefully told me that we needed to find another companion for the journey. Six men were a bad omen, every child in Bhutan knew that. A group should never consist of six men. Years ago six young lads from Thimphu had had the most terrible experiences after going up to the lake above the monastery at Tango. They had lost their way, and four of them had been found weeks later in Punakha half-starved and crazy; the other two had evidently lost their lives.

What were we to do? The only alternative was to start looking for another companion for the journey. I didn't feel like letting the caravan get any bigger, but we had no other choice. The next morning there was excitement: Tshering arrived at the meeting place without the promised seventh man. He had worked out that we were in fact seven; the horseman would protect us from the bad omen of travelling in a group of six. Did I also think that we could also count the horse driver in our numerology? Of course I did. Tshering was reassured.

We didn't set off until the afternoon, driving to Semthoka to begin our trek there. Four pack horses with their driver were waiting for us. One of the mares was leading a foal.

One often sees foals travelling with pack horses. The young animals don't carry any baggage; this is how they get used to the way of life, discipline and duties of a pack horse. The small Himalayan horses carry two woven baskets that hang down on either side of a wooden saddle. The animals are loaded with up to 60 kilos this way; mules can carry even more. Pack horses are their owners' most valuable property. A full-grown horse costs 15,000 *ngultrum*, and a mule up to 25,000 *ngultrum*.

Our guide Sonam showed us the way up to the monastery of Talakha, from where one can see Thimphu to the south, spread out majestically across a mountain ridge. 'Only one hour, if we take the short cut'. We might even make it before the gathering monsoon clouds burst.

The short cut led through a dense bamboo thicket; we then crossed several streams and climbed over rocks, so that it started to look as if this was hardly the quickest way of getting to the monastery. A sudden heavy downpour prepared us for the coming days of trekking during the high monsoon. After more than two hours, we finally reached the monastery, soaked to the skin. It was dark before our horses finally arrived, carrying our sleeping bags and a second, dry, set of underwear.

Friendly monks allowed us to spend the night in the entrance area of the monastery; we were also allowed to use the monastery kitchen, thereby avoiding having to pitch our tents in the rain. We were warned that the hulking black dogs that ran about the monastery had a reputation for being especially loud and aggressive; even the 50-metre walk to the outside lavatory could be very dangerous at night. Until two o'clock in the morning there was loud growling and barking all around us, then finally they fell silent. We, along with the monks, the dogs and no doubt our pack horses seemed finally to be able to settle down for a couple of hours' sleep. Only the pattering of the rain filled the pitch dark night with its steady monotone; the lights of Thimphu had disappeared behind heavy monsoon clouds.

The next morning there was uproar. 'Tiger, tiger!' Out of breath, the horse driver shouted the terrible news to our guide. In the early hours of the morning some predator had killed the foal, who had wandered a few metres away from his mother.

Saddened and deeply upset, the horse driver showed us a hollow in the ground, overgrown with tall grasses and hemp, not 50 metres from the monastery, and only 30 metres from the spot where the dogs were lying about in the morning sun. The predator had first killed the foal with a precisely executed bite to the neck, and had then proceeded to tear open the left side of its belly. The dead animal's liver and intestines lay next to it; that night the big cat would return and satisfy its hunger. Why the dogs had not started barking we would never know.

From the tracks we found in the sandy soil we concluded that it must have been a leopard; the pawprints in the soft earth were too small for a tiger, although it was quite possible to come across a tiger even here, only half a day's walk from the capital Thimphu.

Bhutan's gigantic national parks are connected to each other by protected land corridors, which allow Bhutan's stable tiger population to make extensive forays from the sub-tropical south up into the mountains. Tigers have even been sighted and photographed at Trumshing-La, at just under 4,000 metres Bhutan's highest road pass. There have also been repeated tiger sightings near the monasteries of Tango and Tsheri, only 25 kilometres from Thimphu. Today Bhutan is the country with the healthiest living conditions for the Royal Bengal Tiger, which everywhere else in the Indian subcontinent is under severe threat and on the verge of becoming extinct.

Leopards are far more common than tigers and can be found almost everywhere in the kingdom. Like his darker-coloured relative, the panther, the spotted leopard who had killed our foal that night lives in woodland throughout the high-lying areas of the kingdom, between the Indian plain and the alpine forests. The habitat of the most impressive of these great cats only begins higher up: in summer the rare snow leopard makes forays beyond the treeline into the high pastures above 5,000 metres.

None of this comforted the horse driver. He was grieving for his foal. I couldn't tell whether this grief was really for the material loss he'd suffered, or whether it was for the death of the young animal that had been so full of life only the day before. Bhutanese are easily grief-stricken by the death of an animal, for all are part of an eternal chain of reincarnation.

'Bad for the horse, but good for our environment', is what the Prime Minister *Lyonpo* Yeshi Zimba said a couple of days later, when I told him about it during a conversation about tourist development. Bhutan's unique biodiversity, he told me, was the pride of the nation, and important capital for lasting development that respected the environment and nature. The horse owner would be financially compensated for his loss; in modern, environmentally-friendly Bhutan there were laws to deal with cases such as his.

The caravan driver told me that in former times they would have laced the foal's body with poison. The next night the leopard would have paid for his visit to the carcass with his life. Today even the horse owner knew that hunting and killing big cats and other wild animals in Bhutan was forbidden. He would hold a small *puja* with the monks in order to bid farewell to the dead foal. In Buddhist Bhutan, respect for animals demands such a ceremony.

And it is true that in recent decades Bhutan has undergone a remarkable transformation. The need to protect nature and its diversity of species has not only been enshrined in law, it has also become firmly entrenched in the Bhutanese consciousness. The Third King was known to be an enthusiastic big-game hunter, and died during a safari in East Africa. His son has voluntarily given up hunting, and offers his people an example of how to respect life. Hunting is now forbidden everywhere, even to tourists who are prepared to pay high prices for trophies of rare animals like blue sheep, which are to be found in Bhutan in considerable numbers. A debate has even flared up over fishing. Though permitted in principle, it is strictly regulated by the issuing of fishing permits, while the killing of the inhabitants of Bhutan's crystalline streams and rivers has become increasingly stigmatised.

A long climb led us up into the high mountain pastures of the Dagala mountain range. A good thousand metres uphill brought us to the edge of the treeline, a pioneer zone where rhododendron bushes, gnarled junipers, birches and pines struggled against the wind, the cold and the rocks. Here and there long-stemmed edelweiss offered a foretaste of the delights that lay before us, of days spent crossing the high mountain pastures.

'*Ha Gyello*' we cried in transports of joy, when at midday we crossed the pass at 4,000 metres. It means 'peace to the earth and to the universe' and was accompanied by laying a stone on the improvised *chorten* (stone pyramid), covered with prayer flags that had been tattered by the wind.

We camped at 4,200 metres. We had left Thimphu only twenty-four hours before, and climbing so rapidly to such heights is not without its dangers. We took diamox, a drug with a dehydrating effect which can help prevent altitude sickness. Headaches and insomnia failed to materialise, though the altitude compensates you for these with intense and fascinating dreams. Diamox ensures that these never become too overwhelming, by forcing you out into the cold and rainy mountain night every four or five hours to relieve yourself.

In the early morning the rain let up. We wandered over broad pastures where herds of yaks spend the summer months. All about us were small waterfalls, with crystalline water in their streams even during the monsoon season, and a dozen small lakes. It was a truly sacred landscape. The mountains are its protectors; neither streams nor lakes should be disturbed, dirtied or desecrated.

At midday we rested in a high mountain pasture. Nearby a low stone building huddled against the landscape, offering as little surface area as possible to winter snowfalls. The herdsman's most precious belongings were gathered around the fireplace: a large wooden pestle, in which to prepare butter tea, and yak meat cut into strips and hung up to dry and be smoked. Both are part of the staple diet of every Bhutanese, though they prefer to leave the killing of animals to others. Two shy herdswomen watched us curiously as we ate rice and vegetables with chilli. The only man living in the pasture bore his fate written on his face; his lop-sided and crooked cheekbones, his toothless mouth and the scars that covered his face all told the story of a moment of carelessness. As a small child he had wandered out of his mother's sight just long enough for an irascible yak to deliver a terrible kick to his pretty, boyish face.

That afternoon we headed off for the 4,800-metre pass, the highest along our route, which we crossed nimbly and in a south-westerly direction towards the pastures of Dagala. Before us opened a truly breathtakingly beautiful landscape: starting at almost 5,000 metres, the valley gently sloped away towards the horizon. Below us lay two dozen small shepherds' huts, which, together with several herds of yaks and a series of crystalline lakes, presented what had to be one of the most beautiful views anywhere in Bhutan. We decided to stay.

We also decided to inspect one of the supposedly thousand lakes a little more closely. Despite the ban on disturbing holy water by throwing stones or shouting loudly, Fabian, Sangay and Tshering organised a stone-skimming competition. I cautiously asked whether the gods that watched over these lakes and mountains might punish us for our lack of respect with lightning or hailstorms, but even our Bhutanese friends, normally so very superstitious, laughingly brushed aside such worries.

Tshering and Sangay climbed to the next lake up. Ten minutes later the clouds burst and a thunderstorm descended, whose intensity exceeded any monsoon rains I have ever experienced. The two lads returned from their expedition soaked to the skin, their faces downcast.

After a damp night of steady monsoon rain, dawn roused the yaks who had lain down for the night in the meadow between two stone huts. Yakherders tether their calves in an enclosure every evening; this ensures that their mothers remain nearby. In the morning herdswomen enter the enclosure with small wooden tubs and slowly untie each calf, who immediately runs to his mother. He is allowed a couple of sucks from his mother's udder before he must make way for the herdswoman, who squats down, grips the tub between her thighs and milks about half a litre of marvellous creamy, sweet yak milk. Only then is the calf allowed to return, and the mother yak and her child spend the rest of the day together in the idyllic surroundings of the mountain pastures.

A milk yield of a litre and a half per yak seems pretty wretched next to the yields of highly bred alpine dairy cows. Nevertheless, their large herds of usually a hundred or more animals mean that the yakherders of Bhutan's mountain pastures are able to produce a relatively large amount of cheese and butter, *dahi* (a kind of yoghurt) and sour milk. The cheese is cooked in large copper kettles, with linen cloths to skim off the whey, and then wrapped in cloths and pressed between heavy stones. It is then cut into small cubes, threaded onto pieces of string and hung above the fire to smoke. After several weeks the cubes of cheese have become non-perishable and hard as rock, and a valuable source of food for mountain farmers during the winter months. *Chugo* is then sold in the markets. This method of preparation may well be of interest to dentists, for anyone inadvertently biting too soon into such cheese risks losing a tooth. The rock-hard cubes have to be held in the mouth and passed between the cheeks for twenty or thirty minutes, before body heat and a liberal coating of saliva finally make them soft enough to be chewed. Then they taste marvellous, of summer meadows.

On the meadow in front of the stone hut, a father and his daughter were spinning a thread made out of yak hair. They walked for hours together with the big wooden spindle, the father glancing benevolently at his eighteen-year-old daughter, who already had a baby herself. He spent the summers up here with his two daughters, four grandchildren and both sons-in-law, while his wife remained in the valley and looked after the family home.

Soon enough thread had been spun to braid the fine threads into a thin rope on a wooden winch. Every gesture, every movement of their hands had been handed down over centuries. Today his daughter was being initiated into the art of rope-making. They changed tools again; now each of these two thin cords was attached to another spindle, and the four ends of the cords stretched over a distance of about 50 metres, after which father and daughter bound each of the two lengths into a plait with skilful, swinging movements of the spindle. Finally these two long pieces of cord were braided together. The rope was ready; strong enough to tether a powerful bull yak or to secure a tarpaulin against a storm.

Almost 70 per cent of Bhutan's population are subsistence farmers. They produce most objects for everyday use as well as virtually all their food themselves; thus their output corresponds to their personal needs. There is little space for marketable products or a money economy. There is also a lack of buyers and marketplaces in such a thinly-populated country.

The six of us had reached the end of the route. The horseman unloaded our baggage and returned over the mountain path with the remaining four horses. He was still grieving for his foal. Six men should never try doing anything together.

The Potent Caterpillar

Bhutan's traditional medicine remains a secret

Yes, he said, he had four horses; but he couldn't rent them to me for the trek from Thimphu to Lingshi. He had no horseman to go with them, and he wasn't able to accompany the caravan himself.

Tashi stubbornly refused to accept the job he would otherwise have been so glad to take. There was still snow on the passes, so he would have to reckon on four days to get there and three back. A week altogether; and right now, he said, he just couldn't get away.

In a few days' time the government would announce when the official harvest of the legendary cordyceps could begin. For four weeks, every available man and woman would swarm up to the high valleys along the flanks of the Jomolhari, Jichu, Drake and Tsherim Kang, abandoning their traditional daily work to seek their fortune.

Buyers are prepared to pay up to 50 *ngultrum* for a single cordyceps fungus. If he's lucky, a mushroom hunter might find twenty fungi on a single day, in other words, earn a thousand *ngultrum*. Red *doma* paste dripped out of the corner of Tashi's mouth as he imagined the riches he would soon be raking in.

Realising this, I changed my strategy. I would pay him 5,000 *ngultrum* all in, if he would accompany me with three horses to Lingshi. A sure 5,000 against the dream of a big haul of fungi. After an hour of elaborate estimations and calculations, we agreed on 5,500. In any case we could actually reach Lingshi in three days. Tashi was now suddenly in a hurry, for the sooner he had his horses back in their stable, the sooner he'd be able to start mushroom hunting.

Cordyceps Sinensis (caterpillar club fungus) is one of about 350 herbal remedies that are used in traditional Bhutanese medicine. In *Dzongkha* the strange fungus is called *yartsa goenbub*, 'grass in summer – worm in winter'. A yakherder in Lingshi also once convincingly explained to me that this creature was indeed a caterpillar in winter and a blade of grass in summer.

For hundreds of years, cordyceps has been used in Chinese and Tibetan traditional medicine as a miraculous tonic, whose curative properties can not only enable remarkable sporting achievements and conquer cancer, but also restore virility to the impotent. 'Stronger than Viagra', is what the pharmacist at the Institute for Traditional Medicine told me.

In the 1990s China's track and field athletes smashed the world long-distance record for women. As many as fifteen set international records at national championships. At first, officials were suspected of having allowed false timekeeping. Soon, however, the miraculous records set by the Chinese women's team were explained: the women had been given daily doses of cordyceps for months. The substances it contained were quickly put on the doping lists, and the records annulled.

The Bhutanese clean and dry the peculiar combination of caterpillar and fungus. They then grind the substance and swallow it with a glass of *ara*, the local spirit. Cordyceps is sometimes also put into *ara* and drunk only weeks later.

No one can explain to me whether the restorative substances are contained in the dead caterpillar or the fungus that grows out of it. The caterpillar of a species of moth ingests the spores of the fungus, which it emits into the air in a series of small explosions as it ripens. The affected caterpillar lives a little while longer, burrowing into the earth along the treeline of the high forests. The fungus then begins to grow from the tail end of the caterpillar's body, and can almost reach the same length as the caterpillar itself. This fungal growth pushes through the surface of the earth and looks like a blade of brown grass.

The miraculous and valuable drug is discovered by hunters noticing tiny movements in the caterpillar, which cause the apparent blade of grass to tremble slightly. Only very practised eyes are capable of noticing these minute movements; once it has been discovered, the caterpillar together with the fungus are dug out of the ground and packed into a sealed bag. In the area around the villages of Lingshi, Laya and Thansa, small groups of semi-nomadic people hunt for cordyceps in May and June, while in the meantime the proceeds of their sale can reach as high as 2,000 euros per kilo. In recent years Layaps, Lunanaps and other ethnic groups along the border region with Tibet have grown prosperous since the government legalised the gathering of the potent caterpillar.

Until 2003, this had been limited to employees of the Institute for Tra-ditional Medicine (ITM). Natives of the country were officially obliged to sell their finds only to this institute, receiving for them a price fixed by the state, which was peanuts compared with what they could get for it on the open market. The result was that thousands of mushroom hunters went hunting illegally for cordyceps, many of them coming over the border from Tibet, and most of the harvest was secretly smuggled by middlemen into Tibet and from there into China. Often they were gathered too early, thereby harming the fungus's natural reproduction by airborne spores.

Today all inhabitants of the region are allowed to gather the fungus at strictly regulated times of the year, though they must sell their harvest at regional collecting points, where auctions are held. The first series of these auctions was so successful that Bhutan's ITM was unable to buy a single gram of the highly-prized substance. American, Japanese and Chinese buyers simply outbid the officials from the Ministry of Health. Now 10 per cent of the harvest must be sold at regulated prices to native doctors, while the rest can be sold at market prices to anyone in the world. This has turned simple horse drivers into mushroom hunters, and for a month each year they abandon their horses, children and wives to go looking for cordyceps.

For centuries Bhutan has been known among Chinese doctors as 'mejong', 'land of the medicinal herbs'. The incredible wealth of herbs and plants with curative properties, most of them from the high mountain regions, is the basis for the production of the traditional medicines principally used to treat chronic ailments, but which, as their proponents emphasise, are without damaging side effects.

Tibetan healers are the founders of what today is known as 'traditional Bhutanese medicine'. The tradition, in fact, is not really that old: until the 1950s, medicine in Bhutan was principally the concern of shamans, soothsayers and monks. There were no doctors in the formal sense of the word.

After their country had been occupied by Mao's People's Revolutionary Army, three Tibetan doctors settled in Dechenchoeling near Thimphu and opened their first practice there. Tibetan doctors are both healers and pharmacists in one. They gather their herbs, plants and minerals themselves, and from them produce medicines according to the writings of the so-called Medicine Buddha, diagnose their patients, and treat them with the pills they have made themselves.

Finally the Third King set up the Institute for Traditional Medicine in 1971, in order to give the Tibetan healers a place to work. The clinic is among the most peculiar and successful institutes of its kind. Today it is not only visited by patients but also by tourists, who are astonished to find this fount of peace, calm and benevolent health in the middle of the city.

Ap Davpel is an old man – eighty years old or more, no one knows exactly. In the afternoon he often sits next to the two big prayer wheels in the courtyard of the ITM in Thimphu. Ap is a singer and a musician, one of the most famous in Bhutan, and it is thanks to his love of music that many classic folksongs have not been utterly forgotten.

I liked sitting next to him and turning the prayer wheel. The institute really was one of the quietest and most peaceful places in the city; the power of Bhutanese medicine seemed to radiate from its atmosphere.

Over 2,000 years old, the writings of the medicine Buddha are the basis for the education of traditional doctors, who are called *drungtso* in Bhutan. The ITM's six-year course prepares them for their profession or vocation. There they study the old texts, which are more a collection of experience that has been handed down over the ages than the result of medical research. They learn that for every ailment there are at least two herbally-based medicines, which can only be fully effective if they are prescribed at the weekly *puja* in the Institute's altar room, and if the patient believes in their effectiveness.

No one could explain to me which substances in which herbs are responsible for which effects. All that is handed down is which plants in which proportionate mixture should be used to produce which particular pills or capsules. There have been no attempts at conducting chemical analyses, tests on patients or other kinds or research. After all, they have the experience of three millennia to back them up.

My first visit as a patient to the ITM was hardly spectacular. Traditional medicine specialises in chronic ailments. It complements and reciprocally harmonises with Western medicine, which is available in every regional hospital. In Bhutan, if you have a chronic heart problem with permanent auricular fibrillation and a slightly leaky aortic valve, you go to the ITM and not the surgery.

The *drungtso* took his time listening to my medical history, which, since he spoke no English, had to be translated for him by a young female doctor. I had the slight suspicion that he was listening to it very carefully so he could use it to back up his diagnosis. But then he grabbed hold of my forearm and, smiling kindly and inscrutably, felt my pulse.

'Blood pressure a little on the high side?' he asked. Hadn't I just told him that? Could he really feel my high blood pressure with his fingertips? He looked at my tongue: 'You are very weak, especially the kidneys.' My Chinese doctor had told me the same thing five years ago, as I was waiting for the results of a test on my heart condition. But in the traditional medicine of China, Bhutan and Tibet, heart and kidneys belong together.

On a piece of paper the doctor jotted down some notes in *Dzongkha*. Apart from 'Doc Martin', I couldn't read any of them. On the way to the dispensary the *drungtso* offered the advice that '50 per cent is your believe', and smiled amiably, without volunteering any information regarding my state of health, his planned treatment or when I should return for my next appointment.

The young female doctor led me to the pharmacy on the other side of the courtyard, next to where the two large prayer wheels stood. We spun both of them. Then she had three plastic bags filled with about a hundred different coloured capsules and tablets each. Three brown capsules in the morning, three black pills at midday, three blue-white capsules in the evening. There were twenty-four different herbs in the latter, she explained, then smiled and said that I should come back in a month.

Treatment, consultation and drugs at the ITM are all free, as is the Western medicine available in Bhutan's conventional hospitals – free even for *chilips*. Patients can choose whichever doctor they want to see, who await their clients in small consultation rooms. There are no equipment, laboratories or complicated admission procedures. Drugs are produced in a small factory right next to the Institute, where 240 different herbs and other mainly vegetable substances are prepared.

Medicinal herbs are dried or turned into medicines or added to herbal baths and used in steam therapy. This involves evaporating a mixture of herbs and water in a simple pressure cooker, to which is attached a plastic hose instead of a valve. This is directed at the affected part of the body, and hot steam covers the painful joint or tired spine for fifteen to twenty minutes. This method has great success with degenerative joints, chronic ear, nose and throat infections and menstruation problems.

In addition, there is therapy with gold or silver needles. A 10-centimetre long needle is heated over a gas flame and pressed into the skin without piercing it at points drawn from classical Chinese acupuncture. Small blisters are the only signs that the surface of the skin has been exposed to intense heat. It is a good method of treating chronic pain.

Bhutanese medicine also makes use of *moxen*, small packets of herbs that are applied to acupuncture points and burned. The resulting heat and the aromatic smoke have curative properties. Traditional Bhutanese medicine also includes the art of bleeding or cupping, and occasionally a kind of 'combination therapy' is used with ancient shamanic cults. Thus a *drungtso* using classical Bhutanese treatments may find on a house visit that chicken's eggs, brought by the local shaman, have been placed beneath his patient's armpits.

After a month I had used up all my tablets. I felt good. Better, in fact, than before. But it wasn't clear whether this was attributable to my way of life in Bhutan – the high altitude, the food – or to the herbal remedies of traditional medicine.

The kindly *drungtso* felt my pulse again, wrote something down in his secret script, drew a couple of signs on his patient's notes and said nothing further about my condition. My questions produced one small clue: the treatment could take a long time. Heart patients needed to take his pills for a year or two if they wanted to derive lasting benefit from them.

On my third visit, two months later, he smiled. 'Blood pressure is now rather on the low side'; but he didn't reveal anything more about my status, although I was now definitely feeling that my state of health had changed. The doctor told me that he could not cure me, but it seemed that my condition had improved; I could feel that for myself. And so it had. For the moment I should keep on taking the pills for at least another year, but perhaps also for the rest of my life. I heard this with relief, for I now felt that these pills had played an important part in the improvement of my health – though whether as a placebo or as a generally effective medicine, I could not tell.

One day I woke up to find a great deal of dark blood in my sputum. I went to see the *drungtso* and waited nervously for an explanation or emergency treatment. I thought of the stomach ulcer I had had, and of some the unpleasant side-effects of medicine I had taken for it, and which I hadn't been taking for some time. As ever, the doctor smiled inscrutably. 'That is poison, it must come out.' He did not think it necessary to take any further action.

Later Uden, the young woman doctor, told me that the *drungtso* would undoubtedly have sent me to be X-rayed at the Western hospital if he had not been certain about the causes of this symptom. Between these two very different schools of medicine, envy and jealousy are unknown; for them the sole criterion is the good of the patient.

And in fact on my visits to the ITM I had the distinct feeling – far stronger than in any Western practice – that the *drungtso* and the *menap* (pharmacist) wanted nothing more than that their patient should get well. It was a good feeling.

Uden was one of the few women to have completed the training to be a *drungtso*. In this mother-of-two's native town of Bumthang, people say that doctors' wives can never descend to the hellish underworld in the chain of reincarnation. For this reason her parents had strongly supported their daughter's decision to enter the six-year course at the ITM. During this time, hours of daily prayer had helped her a great deal to understand the complicated material she had to learn. In this way she was able to ward off the evil that always arises when one tries to do good.

Today Uden is married to a *drungtso*, and the two of them have a very modern, equal marriage; as working parents, they divide between each other the responsibilities of household chores and bringing up children. She would love to take a course in acupuncture, if she could get a grant to do so. Her husband supports her in this, and if she were away would take over the bringing up their son and daughter.

For more than a year now my blood pressure has been normal to low. I have had no chest pains for quite a long time now. My atrium still fibrillates, but the sense of being able to feel each individual irregular pulse has gone. On treks and cycling tours I've felt better and stronger than I have for the last twenty years. I've stopped wondering about what kind of influence the herbal remedies have had on my condition.

When I stop by the Institute for Traditional Medicine, I feel happy and peaceful. I sit down next to the prayer wheels and listen to Ap Davpel when he sings the old songs in his high-pitched voice. I have learned to love this place of peace and healing. Blood has not returned to my sputum. The poison has come out.

Passing out in a Wooden Trough

Bhutanese cinema and the erotics of a
traditional hot stone bath

Standing in the foyer of the only cinema in Thimphu, the lead actor was clearly enjoying his popularity. Even Bhutan's tiny film industry can't get by without stars. *Travellers and Magicians*, the box office hit of 2004, had been playing to mostly packed houses for the last four weeks, and every evening at six o'clock both young and old had thronged the entrance to the cinema.

Tsewang, the young hero of the three-hour epic, came to the screenings almost every day. In Thimphu everyone knows everyone else, and here people stopped to shake his hand, talk with him and clap him on the shoulder. The film has actually had something of a success, and in recent years has been shown at alternative film festivals in Amsterdam, Vladivostok and Munich, where its exoticism has drawn considerable attention.

Nevertheless, filmmaking in Bhutan has at best remained a sideline for a few obsessives, who, while working in the shadow of the biggest film industry in the world based in Mumbai, have managed to pursue their own line both artistically and in terms of content. No one in Bhutan can make a living from making films. The producers and directors are generally high-ranking officials, journalists, or – as in the case of *Travellers and Magicians* – highly-educated lamas. Tsewang is a radio reporter, and tourists know him as the ex-husband of Jamie Zeppa, a Canadian teacher who has written one of the most moving books about Bhutan, the story of her love for, and marriage to, one of her pupils. Today he works at the BBS, the Bhutan Broadcasting Service, and has become the *enfant terrible* of Thimphu's evening scene, as well as, on occasion, a film hero.

The entire crew – actors, camera people, lighting assistants, assistant directors and best boys – were amateurs. They filmed with semi-professional high-definition video cameras, since they had neither the money nor the opportunity to buy celluloid. An actor who in the film plays an old man living together with his beautiful, much younger wife in a remote cabin in the woods, told me that shortage of funds also meant that most scenes could be rehearsed just once and then shot in a single take.

In fact the actor lives in a small farmer's house near Paro, and is a retired civil servant who spent half his life working as a maintenance officer at the Bhutanese embassy in New Delhi. There he had the opportunity to observe the film-mad Indians and the incredible cult of their stars at a time when there existed neither cinema nor television in Bhutan.

It pleased him that I had stopped him in the street and told him I had recognised his face from somewhere. 'Maybe you saw me in the movies,' he smiled, when I asked him where I had seen him before. We ended up having a long conversation over tea and cakes about Bhutan's filmmakers, the magic of a medium that has only been known here for a few years, but also about the love between old men and young women. He himself only had a much younger wife in the film; in real life his wife was the same age as him, and spent three days a week at the market selling her vegetables. He was enjoying retirement, though he didn't receive any pension; when they reached the age of retirement, pensioners received only a one-off payment from the civil service aimed at tiding them over. He had managed the return to life as a subsistence farmer well, and only occasionally abandoned this traditional role – for example, when acting in a film.

Travellers and Magicians tells the story of a young Bhutanese official who takes up his first post in the small village of Chendibji, between Trongsa and Wangdue. At the same time he has also applied for a green card to work in the United States, and receives it only a few weeks after he has taken up his job. To seize this opportunity, he must urgently travel to Thimphu for an interview; but he misses the only bus and has to hitch-hike the 200 kilometres along Bhutan's national highway.

He soon finds himself in the company of other travellers who are also trying to hitch a ride with one of the few cars driving along this lonely stretch of road: a lama on the way to his monastery, an apple farmer trying to get to market, a man with his daughter, who has just finished school and now wants to return to the farm. Meanwhile our hero is at great pains to tell everyone that he is the one in the greatest hurry, for a dream job is waiting for him in the land of unlimited opportunities, where he will earn $5 an hour, not $100 a month as in Bhutan's civil service.

'What will you do in America?' asks the wise monk. 'Pick apples,' replies the young hero. 'Hmmm, that certainly does seem important,' replies the monk, the reply of traditional Bhutanese society to the desires of the young to find their fortunes abroad.

More remarkable than the rather simplistic plot are the stories that are told by the wise monk, which he recounts to the other travellers as they are sitting around the campfire and listening to the holy man all night.

In fact, this is an element peculiar to young Bhutanese cinema: a dash of Buddhist wisdom is added to trivial plots that might even have found a producer in Bollywood. The legends and stories incorporated into the film are generally of a greater profundity than its main plot (the young hero eventually, and inevitably, falls in love with the farmer's daughter and decides not to leave the country after all ...).

But the monk tells a quite different story, which, like an interrupted dream, the film keeps slipping back into when its trivial main plot begins to wear thin. It is the story of an old and less-than-handsome man and his young and stunningly beautiful wife. He has built a log cabin deep in the woods, three days' walk from his native village, and there he lives with her in self-imposed solitude, though safe at least from the advances of the young men of the village, who had constantly been making eyes at his wife.

Then one day a rider passing by the cabin falls from his horse, limps his way to the house and asks for shelter until he has recovered from his injury. 'You can stay one night; tomorrow you have to leave'; the old man senses the trouble that the presence of an attractive young man will bring to his marriage. Days go by. Much to the annoyance of the old man, the young man's injured foot means that he cannot continue with his journey.

At this point Bhutan's nascent film industry demonstrates its ability to produce cinema of the highest quality with very simple means. Sex and eroticism are not only frowned upon in Bollywood but also in Bhutan, where many houses have their walls decorated with erect penises as a symbol of fertility, but where an on-screen kiss would be regarded as obscene.

The old man returns home from working in the woods, and his young wife has prepared a traditional hot stone bath to relax him. A two-metre long wooden trough, half-filled with warm water, stands between two screens improvised with towels. His wife brings a hot stone from the camp-fire, which heats the water to sauna-like temperatures. Then, as she massages her husband's shoulders, her eyes seem to gaze into the distance. At this point the audience realises that the young horseman is hiding behind one of the screens and through a narrow slit is watching the woman knead the day's stress out of her husband's shoulders. Their eyes meet. There is no kissing and no nudity other than the bather's shoulders. And yet the scene crackles with erotic tension.

In the cinema the boisterous, cheering, popcorn-chomping audience with its tinkling mobile phones had suddenly gone extremely quiet. At the beginning of the scene there had been some adolescent laughter and a couple of crude comments, but now you could have heard a pin drop.

Eroticism and sexuality are pretty much repressed in Bhutanese public life, though the society has what might be described as a casual attitude towards relationships. People gossip and joke a lot about who is sleeping with whom, but what really goes on is relegated to a hidden area of extreme privacy. The bath scene in *Travellers and Magicians* breaks with this taboo. But it breaks with it in an enormously sensitive way, one that is not provocative but rather encourages reflection and sympathy. It is an example of cinematic body language brought to perfection, directed by a monk with amateur actors.

The mystical bath with its hot stones offers a perfect setting for great cinematic moments. There are few other instances where mind, body and conscious and unconscious meaning are brought together so harmoniously. For the Bhutanese the hot stone bath is an ancient ritual, which benefits health, hygiene and mind. It is used by both young and old. Rather like a sauna in some parts of Europe, it is pleasantly free from prudery and false modesty. Nudity, which is otherwise banished to the sphere of intimacy, is calmly accepted here, and people help and care for one another without regard for age or sex.

The keeper of the small lodge at Trashi Yangtse told us that older men and women would put a plank bed next to their wooden trough, so that they could lie down together right after their bath. We had no idea how seriously this well-intentioned piece of advice had been meant.

For a *chilip* unfamiliar with the art of this enjoyment, first stepping into a hot stone bath can be an exciting adventure: you sit down naked in a wooden trough filled with bath-warm water. They give you a couple of minutes to acclimatise, then an assistant arrives carrying a glowing hot stone from the nearby hearth between a large pair of iron pincers. It hisses as he drops it into the water at the foot of the trough. A blue plastic screen is placed around the tub, but I was soon so overwhelmed by the experience that I was unable to worry about people peeping in.

The hot stone started transferring its heat to the water. A second and a third followed. I was careful to draw up my legs and not touch the stones with my feet. The temperature of the water kept rising. It was soon hot enough to discourage anyone from getting in who wasn't already. I didn't know how much longer the temperature would keep rising; if it got unbearable, no one would be able to fish the hot stones out. I seemed to have lost the strength to get out of the bath if I needed to.

I felt a mixture of dizziness, fear and pleasantly warming stimulation. The heat wasn't only affecting my body; it was causing my mind to wander – to fairyland, perhaps, or another level of being. I couldn't tell which. I couldn't even say what I was thinking. But as the water got steadily hotter, I found I wanted to stay in it. At some point the temperature stopped rising. Through a veil of steam and dreams I heard someone say, 'Another stone?' Better not, I meant to reply; but couldn't tell whether I'd actually said anything or not.

Twenty minutes later I got out of the trough, and sat down immediately on the wooden edge. I couldn't stand. I was dizzy. Or was I losing my mind?

My companion got ready for her bath, and the water was cooled with a couple of buckets of cold spring water. I was still sitting on the edge of the trough. For twenty minutes I couldn't say anything. Slowly my mind started to find its normal rhythm again. She hadn't said a word, and her closed eyes seemed to be saying 'never mind about me, I'm somewhere else'. Eventually she got out of the trough as well, and immediately fell into my arms. With her hot body slumped lifelessly over mine, I was overcome by a short moment of panic. I called to her but there was no reaction. The fainting fit lasted a good two minutes.

Then we both discovered why the Bhutanese put a camp bed next to the wooden trough. Occasionally the circulation collapses after a hot stone bath. The extreme temperatures send the mind, the will and even the desires off to different worlds, while it is all the heart, lungs and circulation can do to keep the body and its temporarily departed soul standing upright.

Bhutan's filmmakers have done a better job than politicians or tourist agents in bringing foreigners closer to the Bhutanese soul. The scene with the wooden trough shows a kind of eroticism that can only be experienced in this kingdom above the clouds.

The box office hit of 2005 tells the true story of a prince's daughter from eastern Bhutan. Monks and astrologers had determined that a great *chorten* had to be built in order to drive away a harmful demon. *Chorten Kora*, today one of the most important places of pilgrimage in the border area between Bhutan and Arunachal Pradesh, is the title of the film version of a wistful story of faith and love. The whole of Thimphu was talking about this film when I went to see it with Jigme, my neighbour. She would give me a whispered translation of the most important dialogue, for the film is shot entirely in *Dzongkha*.

We watched as, accompanied by some outstanding film music, thousands of people followed the monks' advice and started building the largest *chorten* in Bhutan. The subplot tells the story of the prince's daughter whose father organises a horse race to find a suitable husband for his princess. There are plenty of laughs and the bride, who sings with a marvellously beautiful voice, fortunately falls in love with the right man – that is, the one who later wins the race.

The time has now come for the two of them to be alone together. In Bhutan people don't wait for the wedding night. Rather the other way round: if two lovers have finally slept together and moved in with each other, they are considered to be married – there are still few people who bother with registered marriages and wedding ceremonies. His Majesty the King lived together with his wives for many years, and even had several children by them, before he formally married his queens.

Doubtless, though, to the great disappointment of audiences, the princess's tutelary divinity appears to her just at the moment when she means to share her life with her beloved. He shows her that another fate has been determined for her, and that she must renounce her night of love.

The next day, high-ranking monks tell her father what the oracle has demanded: his maiden daughter must be walled up in the now almost completed *chorten*. It is the only way to overcome the demon for good. Tears are shed, but the brave young woman is determined to follow the advice of the holy men and her own divinity. In a deeply moving scene, she strides up the *chorten* followed by a large crowd of people, then kneels down to meditate on top of the building while she is walled in. All this really happened in the 17th century; her remains lie to this day inside the gigantic *chorten*.

My eyes had become moist, and the audience in the cinema had gone quiet. All of us were in the spell of a drama played with great seriousness and emotion. Later I asked Jigme, a young wife and a mother of two,

'What would you have decided to do if the monks had suggested such a plan to you the day before your wedding?' Without hesitation she replied, 'Of course I'd have sacrificed myself if it would have helped the people around me.' The next day I asked my 22-year-old secretary the same question. She too would have let herself be walled up.

The most popular film of 2006 showed that Bhutanese cinema can also be extremely funny. *Druk Ghe Goem* ('Guest of the Thunder Dragon'), announced with great fanfare by both of Thimphu's newspapers and on television, happened to be the first Bhutanese film with a foreign actor in it. That alone was reason enough to see it.

An American tourist, played to great if unintentional comic effect by a young man with blond hair and a black beard, gets lost on a trekking tour between Gasa and Laya. With his ankle sprained, he huddles miserably in the middle of a wood where he is almost eaten by a bear, and where he is reduced to crying for help.

Tshomo, a young herdswoman from Laya who lives with her herd of yaks on a lonely mountain pasture, hears his cries, saves the *chilip*, and soon takes him under her wing in every sense of the word. Denkar, her younger sister, helps out with her few scraps of English. Soon, injuries are healing and hearts are enflamed. However, evil officials eventually send the guest away as his visa has run out – a serious offence in a country where visitors are obliged to spend at least $200 a day. But a kindly travel agent finally manages to have the American let back into the country, and nothing stands in the way of a happy ending to the story.

With usual Bhutanese politeness, the media have heaped ovations upon the lead American actor. But I can't get over the impression that the young man walked into the role quite by chance – it shouldn't be considered one of his great acting achievements. By contrast, the two Bhutanese actors, the well-known Dorji Wangmo and the newly-discovered Pema Dechen, play their parts with great verve, authenticity and conviction. As members of the mountain tribe of Layaps they are utterly believable, and Tshomo moves around the yak-hair tent of the mountain nomads as if she had lived there all her life.

Outside the cinema, while young Bhutanese women chattered effusively over the hero's blue eyes and blond-black hair, foreigners found themselves reflecting on what could actually happen if they got lost in Gasa's high mountain forests.

Incidentally, while Bollywood has been marketing European, African and American tourist centres for years, thereby initiating a veritable travel boom to these destinations, the Indian film industry has so far been refused permission to shoot in the Land of the Thunder Dragon.

'We would never agree even to a single commercial', a high-ranking official in the Department of Tourism confided to me. He defended this position by saying that the quality of Bollywood films, their content and their 'message' did not suit Bhutan. Anyone who has seen Bhutanese films will agree with him.

The Naked Men of Bumthang

The monastery where tourists stay up until midnight

If they worked out you were a foreigner you'd be paying six euros for a portion of *momos* (five cheese pasties). People were cleaning the worst dirt off a building site and for the next three days calling it a 'hotel'. With night temperatures around freezing point, drivers and guides slept in the tour bus because every bed in town was taken. The hotels were so overbooked that you could see the beads of sweat stand out on their owners' foreheads.

It was high season in Bumthang. The fateful week at the end of October was leading to the classic excesses of overheated demand. Elderly high-ranking officials, who were now trying their hand as hoteliers, were turning into nervous, grasping old men. The place was dominated by a fleet of buses, minivans, pick-ups and other vehicles, all of which had been rented out by tourists. For a week the delightful peace of the Bumthang valley disappears; a place where, in the 1970s, some Swiss aid workers found themselves feeling so at home that two of them married Bhutanese women and settled down.

Only 15 per cent of tourists to Bhutan manage to travel this far east. The prospect of three days of driving along poor roads in minibuses with bad suspension – and another three days back – means that most decide against an expedition into the Bumthang Valley, 2,800 metres above sea level. Except for during this strange week in October.

'Everyone goes crazy, but it's all over in a couple of days,' says Fritz Maurer, who is these days more Bhutanese then Swiss, and who has both followed and helped shape the development of tourism in his new homeland from its first tottering steps. Despite all the modern, comfortable hotels that have recently been built, his Swiss Guest House is still considered by those in the know to be *the* place to stay on a visit to Bumthang. His eldest son Tshering is now running the business together with his Bhutanese wife. 'We went to school together, but it wasn't until much later that we realised that there was something more between us', says the proud father of a small son.

In the meantime he had spent nine years in Switzerland and completed his military service, although at the time he barely understood any Swiss German. He used this time to learn something else as well: 'I was assigned to the field kitchen, and we cooked for 100, 200, sometimes 500 men. No one could imagine doing that here, but it helps an awful lot if you're trying to run a hotel.' He trained as a cheese maker, like his father Fritz, who in the early 1970s used this qualification to set up dairies in Gogona and Bumthang, increased the milk yields of the cows by crossing them with other species, and thereby became responsible for the fact that there are now several outstanding cheeses in Bhutan, varieties of Gouda and Emmental. Even though only small quantities of them are produced to this day, and the consumers are principally tourists and expatriates, there have been real economic benefits for farmers participating in this programme.

Fritz Maurer was also godfather to the development of the *boukhari*, a small metal oven used all over Bhutan that has replaced open hearths in thousands of peasant houses and which is still produced in Bumthang today. Maurer is also to be thanked for the fact that you can buy delicious unsweetened apple juice, as well as three extremely good varieties of honey. In a country where eating honey was until recently considered a grave sin since it was seen to involve stealing from bees, this was, apart from anything else, a remarkable ideological feat. The king is said to have looked into the matter personally and convinced himself that it involved no harm to the bees. Only then was the green light given to the beehives.

Maurer's remarkable qualities become even clearer when presented with a glass of Red Panda. Printed on the bottle's red label is the word 'Weissbeer' in mixed Anglo-German, and the only beer to be brewed in Bhutan is indeed a 'white' or wheat beer. The microbrewery in Bumthang is well-known among beer lovers, and for years has been unable to keep up with the demand for this speciality. Cautiously and with typical Swiss foresight, his son Tshering Maurer has set about extending the brewery and has been testing out Bhutan's first draught beer, needless to say in the Swiss Guest House. Given that an excellent 'Chrüter' is to be had there, a schnapps distilled from aniseed, fennel, gentian, cinnamon and medicinal herbs, as well as fondue for supper and home-made strawberry and raspberry jam, it comes as no surprise to find the achievements of Maurer and his family so astonishing.

The King has granted him Bhutanese citizenship and the honorary title of *dasho* for his services. Most people who meet him don't realise that this elderly man squatting eating chilli rice on a small carpet in the kitchen isn't in fact a native Bhutanese. Fritz speaks *Dzongkha* and English; his Swiss German is a little rusty. He has sent his children to school in Switzerland, but they have all come back and are more Bhutanese than Swiss, combining in a remarkable way the positive characteristics of both cultures.

Anyone managing to get hold of one of the comfortable rooms in the Swiss Guest House during the monastic festival, whose furnishings are strongly reminiscent of those in Swiss Alpine Club cabins, may consider themselves lucky.

There are at least five dozen *tsechus* (monastic festivals) in Bhutan every year, spread over the months from September to June. The masked dancers pause only in high summer, when the monsoon rains would make an outdoor performance impossible. But tourists from all over the world throng to the Paro *tsechu* in spring, the Thimphu *tsechu* in September, and especially the Jambay Lhakhang Drup in October.

A long time ago the masked dance of the small monastery of Jambay moved from the inner courtyard to a special field next to the monastery itself because there wasn't enough space for the constantly growing

number of visitors in the monastery courtyard, where *tsechus* had tradi-
tionally been held. For these three days, the area behind the ancient monastery of Lhakhang turns into a tent city of countless market stalls. Traders
cook over dozens of small hearths, tables and chairs stand beneath plastic
sheeting, farmers' wives with shining red cheeks offer *momos*, *somoza*,
papard, breaded chillies or simply rice with *ema datshi*. To accompany it
there is *suja* (salted butter tea) served from thermos flasks, beer and the
fashionable drink Spy – an atrocious imitation wine from Thailand in
an excitingly opaque bottle. The most popular drink is Hit beer, a strong
beer from neighbouring Sikkim which, particularly in rural Bhutan, is
preferred to the other imported beers from India or Singapore.

Next to the food stalls are people selling junk to suit every purse, from
plastic toys for children to glass beads for women, and offering a wealth of
opportunities for young men to ostentatiously pull some banknotes out
of their *ghos* and buy presents for all and sundry. A little distance away
was a small clump of tents from which a loud commotion could be heard.

'Lucky number! Try the lucky number! One, two, three, four, five, six
– lucky number!', a sweating fat man was shouting at the top of his voice.
About a dozen excited punters were crowding round his gaming table, the
youngest of whom can't have been fourteen. They skilfully folded their 10-
and 20-*ngultrum* notes while the crier shook six oversized wooden dice
in a worn-out wooden cup and rolled them vigorously across the table.
'Lucky number!'

By now banknotes were being thrown onto the six fields numbered
from one to six. They were mostly tens and twenties, but the Indian-look-
ing youth, his face sweating from chewing too much *doma*, pushed onto
the number six a tightly-folded pink note – 500 *ngultrum*, the largest
banknote in the kingdom. A murmur went through the crowd.

The crier lifted his cup to reveal three sixes, two fours and a two. Quick
as a flash, the fat man's assistant raked up the notes sitting on numbers
one, two, three and five with the most poker of poker faces; they fell into
a black plastic bag already bulging with banknotes. The two fours mean
that stakes placed on the four are doubled, while the three sixes mean the

500 *ngultrum* on the six is paid back three times. The sweating gambler quickly gathered up his winnings of 1,500 *ngultrum* – for many here, more than a month's wages.

Gambling is permitted in Bhutan only on certain festival days and as part of a *tsechu*. The rules are simple, the proportion between what the bank makes and pays out in winnings half-way fair, and at least transparent. A Western observer calculated that over the space of half an hour about 80 per cent of the takings were paid out again, a fact that tempted the author of these lines to try his luck. Gambling *chilips* are a novelty, and cries of excitement rang out; 20 *ngultrum* on six, the number that had already caused such a furore with the 500 *ngultrum* note. 'Lucky number!' the cup was raised – 'number six!' – I had won 40 *ngultrum* at the first try. I hastily thrust the three notes into my pocket and resolved to resist all further temptations of the gaming board.

But the real reason people visit the Jambay Lhakhang Drups are more personal than this. The festival is a popular marriage market among the locals. Only a deeply religious minority earnestly follow the three days and nights of the monks' dancing. Boys and girls of marriageable age – that is, from fifteen to twenty – spend most of their time at the market, where in large and small groups they stroll up and down among the stalls, now and then stopping at one to drink a Hit beer and show off how macho they are, or to suck lasciviously at a bottle of Spy, as they imagine the fashionable girls in distant Thimphu do.

If it's true that human beings are more likely to find mates at full moon, the Jambay Lhakhang Drup offers the proof. At some point, a good many of the boys and girls find a suitable partner and together escape the commotion of the market to head off into the silvery moonlight. Even if at the beginning it seems as though the groups of girls have merely been giggling at the antics of the boys, at some point during the night the eyes of two of them meet, and together they flee the general commotion of the undecided, to begin, at some quiet spot in the cool night, a serious dialogue of body and soul. Thus it is that many marriages in central Bhutan have their origins near the monastery of Jambay, beneath a full moon in October.

But tourists also have personal reasons for coming to Jambay. None of them would ever admit that the strange dance that takes place around midnight in the courtyard of the monastery has had any influence on their travel plans. They aren't twenty any more; closer, perhaps, to sixty – and yet for three nights in a row *chilips* from all over the world start gathering at about six in the evening to get the best places and to wait for a dance that is radically different from the usual masked dances of Bhutanese monastic festivals.

Long ago, some monks wanted to build a monastery in the small village of Nabche, south of Trongsa. But every night demons came and destroyed their laborious day's work, and the monks had constantly to start again from the beginning. To ensure their Sisyphean labour might finally come to an end, the monks came up with a cunning ruse: they let it be known that at night they would be dancing naked in a clearing in the wood, many miles distant from where they were building the monastery. The demons were fascinated at the prospect, and, filled with curiosity, followed the monkish strippers, forgetting all the while that they were supposed to be destroying the monastery. Thus by their regular nocturnal dances the monks finally succeeded in completing the building.

The so-called naked dance of monks commemorates this event, and has long been plugged as a special attraction by the monastery's tourist marketing. Far be it from me to suggest that this is why 85-year-old Japanese ascetics, 75-year-old American women with facelifts, or 65-year-old pot-bellied Germans are drawn here every year to spend hours sitting on the damp grass, spending the night in tents, provisional accommodation, farmhouses or building sites after having driven hundreds of kilometres through the Himalayas over bad roads. But the fact is that they were all there.

At six o'clock the first hundred or so tourists started gathering at the festival grounds, staked their claims right in front of the roped-off dance space, sat down on the wet grass and waited. For the dances would not begin until eight o'clock. But they wanted to be right at the front. Two hours later, when the number of *chilips* had grown to at least 400, a dance begins that lasts 45 minutes and ends with a fire ceremony.

For the first fifteen minutes the cameras' clicking shutters seemed to set the rhythm, with electronic flashes flickering in three-second bursts across the festival site, as if the kindly Thunder Dragon were present himself. After an hour the batteries were starting to run out, and the moonlight was gradually winning out against the storm of flashes.

At nine o'clock the guides started encouraging their clients to stay. They were tired of waiting, and they were cold. The guides assured their guests that they simply could not go home before the naked dance. At half-past nine the night claimed its first victim.

'We didn't come for the naked monks' dance anyway,' the first two dozen tourists headed home exhausted; their reason sounded decidedly politically correct. And in any case photography was forbidden. By about half-past ten more than half the tourists had left the festival ground, while in the meantime a boisterous crowd of local market-goers had taken their places.

At midnight there were only about fifty *chilips* left when a rumour started going about that everyone should move to the monastery court-yard, since that was where the legendary naked monks would dance. The crowd was not nearly as big as had been feared it might have been. In the middle of the courtyard, which could hold about 200 people, a white circle had been painted, in the middle of which a couple of wooden logs waited to be lit.

It was clear that only the locals knew what was really going on. We tourists sat down politely on the stone floor and waited again. At about half-past twelve our thin ranks were swelled by a large number of Bhuta-nese who suddenly crowded into the tiny courtyard. Five policemen cor-doned off the only entrance and locked the gates. Outside hundreds of fists drummed angrily against the gate. My neighbour, a young female offi-cial from the Royal Audit in Thimphu, explained to me that 'They do no allow those in who are not properly dressed.' Evidently, while the women were all dressed in pretty *kiras*, the men were wearing jeans and T-shirts that made fashionable references to Marlboro, the anti-AIDS campaign or Che Guevara, and had to stay outside. They weren't, however, going to put up with it. The hammering on the gates sounded ever more threatening, and several *chilips* looked frightened. Then there was a splintering noise and the wooden lock broke, giving the policemen just enough time to withdraw to secure positions.

A tsunami of improperly dressed young men burst into the already overcrowded courtyard. At this point panic threatened to break out, and tourists who had been valiantly defending their places near the front of the white circle fled fearfully to the further corners of the courtyard. The wave of people happened to carry me to a point right next to the chalk circle from where I would have the best view of the coming spectacle.

After about a quarter of an hour everyone had calmed down again, and about 400 people were now jammed together in the courtyard. Most of the tourists had lost their privileged places; I had been lucky.

The wooden logs were doused in kerosene and lit. Finally a man with cymbals cleared a way through the mass of people. He beat out a rhythm for the dancers, but was not, as was normally the case, a monk himself.

And then they came: the extraordinary bodies for whom Bumthang had had to suffer this week of madness. Their only piece of clothing, which protected the dancers' anonymity, was the white cloth wrapped around their heads which masked dancers wear beneath their wooden masks. Small slits in them for the eyes and mouth allowed for sufficient freedom of movement.

The first one stumbled across the chalk circle, attempted a couple of dance movements and then fell into the burning fire. The second and third dancers pulled their colleague, obviously very drunk, from the pile of logs. Eventually fifteen of them started moving around the fire. It couldn't be described as dancing. Why were these monks drunk, and why couldn't they dance?

We allowed out attentions to be occupied by more pressing concerns. For they *were* naked. To relieve male European readers of the nervousness they might feel at the description of an African fertility ritual, I can report that the dancers' nether parts were thoroughly proportional to the average size of the Bhutanese.

What so many tourists and locals – and demons as well, according to the legend – had spent so much trouble coming to see had been hidden by some of the dancers behind and artfully arranged bushel of yak hair. Others left theirs uncovered to swing modestly about, while others had taken a lesson from the country-wide anti-AIDS campaign and presented themselves properly protected by a dark-blue condom. Two of the condom wearers had guessed that the tourists had probably come to see something a little more impressive and put a cucumber down the limp rubber in order to increase their size. And as a result they did look a little more imposing.

But there was no doubt about it: these brave men could not dance. And this could not be attributed to the copious amounts of alcohol they had evidently drunk before coming on stage. In a decidedly unromantic manner, they performed gymnastic exercises in groups of two, three and four that made perfectly clear what they would have wanted to be up to if it had not been so cold, if there hadn't been so many spectators and if their pricks hadn't shrunk almost minimalistically to a few wrinkled centimetres. What the monks were doing here was pretty vulgar.

Monks? My neighbour from the Royal Audit straightens me out: for years the naked dance hasn't been performed by monks at all, who, it seems, had stopped enjoying it once it started turning into a piece of commercialised voyeurism. The local folk dancers sent their male members in order to 'maintain the tradition'. Whether the monks, as is rumoured, occasionally perform their ritual behind closed monastery doors is not clear.

The fifty remaining tourists were more or less speechless; it was clear that they had been expecting something different. The whole sorry business was over by half-past one. Nevertheless at breakfast they would be able to tell the lightweights who didn't stay up that evening how much they had missed. And the legend of the naked, dancing monks of Bumthang would ensure that next year every chicken coop would be packed with tourists during this crazy week in October.

With a Dagger in his Belly
and His Hands in Boiling Oil

Only the dancing shaman's wife can understand him

The invitation to the *terda* sounded so incredible that at first I thought it was a joke. But Tshering seriously assured me that no *chilip* had ever witnessed this ceremony, in which the dancer falls into a trance and thrusts a sword so deeply into his innards that anyone trying to pull it out would have to use all his strength.

The farmer's house stood only a short distance from the road through the 3,700-metre high Dochu-La, which runs east from Thimphu through central Bhutan. We were soon sitting pleasantly round the living room of the house, with its half-timbering and walls of packed clay.

The host's son showed me his constantly cheerful six-month-old son. He was unable to hide how passionately in love he was with his beautiful young wife. Some young men in their mid-twenties were taking turns to look after the small children with great warmth and tenderness, holding them in their arms or simply carrying them around with them as if it were the most natural thing in the world.

As a foreign guest I have the honour of tasting all the specialities of the local schnapps. I particularly liked *fried ara*. Corn schnapps, distilled using simple implements from wheat or barley mash, typically has fresh scrambled eggs added to it and stirred in. This makes the drink both more nutritious and more powerful.

The father of the household, who was to perform the dance, also joined us. He was a simple man in his late fifties, a farmer and a retired non-commissioned officer of the royal bodyguard.

At about eight o'clock the party slowly decamped to a tent that had been built onto the house. Inside was an enormous altar arranged with dozens of artfully shaped decorative pieces made of dyed butter. Buddhist good luck signs were placed above the altar, *kaddars* (ceremonial shawls) were suspended everywhere, *thankas* (scroll paintings) hung from the walls. The floor had been laid with a large, 10-metre square carpet. On one side the tent was open, and about 300 spectators were already sitting there, among them the neighbouring family who were sponsoring the *terda* this year.

The altar stood along the wall of the house. Opposite it a ceremonial chair had been built of the kind that high-ranking monks use in monastery prayer halls. Right next to it stood a second, similarly decorated chair, where the *lam* had already taken his place together with four monks carrying classical musical instruments: two *dungs*, long, telescope-like horns that produced sounds similar to alpenhorns; a *nga*, a large, hanging drum; two *jalings*, also telescopic, which produced sounds that were like a mixture of trumpets and clarinets; and two *kangdungs*, wind instruments fashioned from human shin bones.

Our host the dancer now joined us in the marquee. Without ceremony, he started putting on his ceremonial robes. He took off his *gho* and, standing half-naked in the tent, started to pull on the yellow, red and green robes, assisted by his wife. They looked similar to the clothes worn by dancers at masked festivals, only he wore no mask. Instead, two elaborately decorated hats stood to one side. His wife explained to me that the hats indicated which god was speaking from him; at first it would be the god of birth, then the god of wisdom, who would be guiding him when he was in a trance. Finally, he put on another belt, into which he thrust a metre-long sword.

By now the sixty visitors to the ritual had calmly and quietly gathered. There were many children and babies among them, for it is believed that the *terda* offers these special blessings and good health. It struck me that, despite the late hour, none of the children were crying or whining or in any way disturbing the remarkable silence of the proceedings. Later, one of the babies fell asleep. The shaman's wife asked her mother to wake the child, for it was supposed to watch and take in the *terda* while its spirit was awake. When the small girl started whining a little, her mother immediately took her outside, for there had to be absolute silence while the possessed man was dancing. After five minutes she returned, and for the rest of the evening the six-month-old baby watched the performance wide-eyed and in silence.

My friends and I had been given places of honour at the front end of the tent, right next to the horns. We were lucky, for there is nothing I like to hear more than the two-part humming of the *dungs*, which causes the pit of one's stomach to vibrate pleasantly.

The dancer was now ready. He had just finished chatting with his neighbour, and now he seemed to concentrate on the beginning of the ceremony. His wife gave the monks a short command, and the latter started praying, accompanied by the deep tones of the horns, the beat of the drum, and an occasional shrill note from the *jalings*.

By now the dancer was breathing deeply; then he opened his mouth very wide, and in the cold of the night one could see his breath fog the air. His eyes were tightly shut, and with his wide-open mouth he seemed to be offering a way into his body for the spirit that would possess him.

Suddenly his whole body started twitching, and shuddered three, then four, then five times, as if being struck by electric shocks. He stuck his arms straight upwards and started breathing heavily, giving out a series of grunts. His eyes were now open, but turned directly upwards, and he seemed to be staring convulsively at the roof. He was trembling from his waist down and gasping for air, and in the meantime had started hyper-ventilating as if afflicted by the pangs of childbirth.

The spectators had fallen utterly silent and were watching the performance with a mixture of calmness and awe. Even the children had been spellbound; but their expressions were relaxed. They seemed to understand that, from it, good would come to them.

The dancer was now wracked by cramps; first he panted out loud, then he struggled for air, before collapsing into the ceremonial chair where the strange transformation would take place. He was now sitting in apparent exhaustion, emitting short, loud breaths. Then he started speaking. Only no one could understand him. What language was he speaking? It was, my friend whispered reverentially to me, Lhasa Tibetan, the language of the learned monks from the centre of the Tibetan lama tradition. But his son assured me that his father did not speak a word of Tibetan. It was only in the trance of the *terda* that he used this language, which was otherwise wholly unknown to him. Only his wife and assistant seemed to understand him. She followed his instructions and gave a few more to the young man who was also assisting, but who could not understand what the entranced man was saying.

He was now calling for *ara*, and his wife brought him a large mug of it from which he drank three deep draughts, again accompanied by stertorous breathing and a constant trembling from his hips down that he seemed unable to control. He took a handful of grains of rice from another assistant, drew his sword and placed the rice on it, rubbed his hands over it, threw some of grains in the air and repeatedly asked his wife how many grains were in the scabbard of his sword. His muttered replies to her answers sounded at times to be agreeing, at other times to be disagreeing, but they were always preceded by a loudly shouted 'ya-ya-ya-ya'. No one could tell me what he was saying. No one could understand him.

The monks prayed and accompanied the unearthly scene on their drums and horns. Sometimes his wife would give them a sign that they should start singing a different prayer. They obeyed; for here it was not the high-ranking *lam* that was in charge, but the dancer who was giving instructions through his assistant.

The possessed man's face bore no resemblance to the farmer I had been eating with two hours before. His lower lip was pressed constantly over his teeth, and his breathing was shallow and extremely fast, though from time to time accompanied by a grunting and hissing that did not sound like human sounds at all. His eyes remained gazing upwards, his forehead was deeply furrowed.

I was starting to understand what the locals had been at great pains to tell me: that dancing before us was not the kindly farmer from next door, but his body possessed by a divinity who was really performing the dance and the ritual. For this creature whirling with astonishing bounds across the carpet no longer had anything in common with the farmer. The wild dance, partly performed on one foot, was accompanied by drumbeats and trumpets. The masked dancers at the *tsechus* are famed for their skilful dances, but these are generally slow and dignified. What was now unfolding before my eyes was an ecstatic spinning, next to which whirling dervishes looked like an elderly couple dancing a slow waltz.

The man was retired and pushing sixty. Exhausted, he finally let himself collapse into his 'throne', asked for *ara* and this time also for milk, then muttered some phrases in Tibetan together with his 'ya-ya-ya-ya'. Despite the enormous physical exertion, there was no sweat on his tense, furrowed forehead.

Several rounds of wild dancing, with refreshment in the short pauses between them, were succeeded by another transformation. This time the other head-dress was brought on, and again it seemed as if he were being taken over by another (divine?) personality. His mouth stood wide open, his body shuddered and trembled, stiffened as if struck by lightning; then he sat down exhausted on a chair. His wife put the second head-dress on his head.

What role was she playing? She was the only one who understood his instructions, and even translated them for the monks. She brought whatever he asked for, smiled calmly when he seemed to be completely beside himself, grunted and groaned, whirled about or collapsed exhausted to the floor. Was she his confidante of many years, were the two of them a team trying to earn a bit on the side with this hocus-pocus? Was she the only one who knew it was all an act, and that the dramatic scenes the audience had been watching for the last two hours were in fact only carefully-rehearsed stunts?

There was no time to think about this. The new god had taken control of the dancer. His assistant handed him a bamboo bow and arrow. Five metres away an egg sat upon the altar. He breathed heavily as he took careful aim, shot – and missed. The dancer drew another arrow, and missed again. Then he missed a third time. It was only with his sixth shot that he hit his target, whose shell, dripping with yolk, was now hanging from the tip of the arrow. His female assistant triumphantly showed it to the astonished spectators.

His next routine was also pretty unsensational. The dancer laid a fine, white *kaddar* on his metre-long sword, as he had already done a dozen times before. Only this time he didn't throw the ceremonial veil onto the altar, but whirled it above his head. He let the feather-light silken cloth float slowly to the floor, picked it up again, and repeated the performance five times until the *kaddar* finally seemed to hang from the roof of the tent, in contradiction of all laws of nature. But it wasn't hard to figure out that the bamboo struts supporting the tarpaulin were covered with splinters and tiny pieces of wood which the gossamer-thin veil could catch on. Western spectators were deeply unimpressed by this supposed miracle.

Outside, near the open side of the tent where most of the spectators were sitting on the ground, a small pile of logs was lit, and a large saucepan about one-quarter filled with oil placed on top of it. The dancer whirled outside and glanced bewildered into the saucepan in which the oil was slowly heating. He then raced tirelessly through the neighbouring building, followed only by his assistant and the sponsor's closest relatives.

After a quarter of an hour he came back, and examined again the fire and the saucepan, in which the oil had in the meantime reached boiling point. Gesticulating wildly and breathing deeply, the possessed man circled the saucepan and, beneath the eyes of the astonished spectators, repeatedly drew up the sleeves of his coloured clothes, apparently in preparation for what was to come.

Finally he placed himself in front of the fire, the flames throwing wild shadows across his face. Beseechingly he raised his arms, then, for a short moment, thrust both his hands into the pan with the boiling oil. For far too short a moment: it at least looked as if he were faking it. But he seemed to guess we had our suspicions, and immersed his hands a second time in the seething liquid, holding them there for several seconds.

He licked the oil running off his fingertips. Was he fighting back pain? How could he not be? The oil was boiling hot, and his hands had been immersed up to the palms; there had been no cry of pain, and no visible injuries. But maybe anyone could do it; in the same way that you can run across hot coals if you have your mind and body under proper control? While I was considering this, the spectators started removing clothes from certain parts of their bodies.

'It will heal all your ailments if he touches you with his oil-soaked fingers,' my host explained to me. In front of me two elderly women pushed their way to the healer; one had bared her shoulder, the other presented first her abdomen to the divinity, then her back. He anointed the exposed parts of the body while blowing on them in panting breaths. 'Ffffh, ffffhhh, ...', his breath hissed between pursed lips onto the affected areas.

Now the children were lining up. Some of them were completely naked; the anointing with oil was supposed to protect them from every kind of illness.

The dancer called for *ara* and milk, threw some rice grains in the air, uttered his 'ya-ya-ya-ya' and spouted Tibetan mantras – or were they instructions to his assistant? For three hours now he had been spinning like a top back and forth across the carpeted floor. Again he drew his sword from his belt, cut at the air, seemed to find his target, then lowered the deadly weapon again, and threw *kaddars* onto the butter sculptures of the altar.

Finally he placed the sword at a 45-degree angle in front of himself, with the tip of the blade pointing at this groin and its hilt resting on the ground. At first there was the mere suggestion that he was gently pressing his lower belly against the sharp blade. He stopped, started again, panted and groaned, grunted and whistled. Perhaps a dozen times he pressed against the steel, a small length of which actually seemed to disappear into his belly.

Finally he got up and now all could see that the sword was sticking into either his belly or groin; his flowing robes meant it was difficult to say exactly which. He took a few steps, grabbed hold of the blade sticking into his innards, then ran to the side of the tent behind his throne and threw himself, with the sword sticking out in front of him, several times and with great energy against the tautly stretched canvas. Did the sword actually disappear a few more centimetres into his abdomen? It seemed to. There was no blood, and even his robes did not seem to have been cut. His expression betrayed great exertion, but no pain.

After this breathtaking attempt to force the sword deeper into his body, he sank onto the throne; and in this sitting position the sword really seemed to be sticking deeply into him. At this point his wife and assistant came back on stage. No one had warned me about what the other spectators seemed to know: the *chilip* would have the honour of drawing the sword out again.

Having fallen back into a trance, the dancer was again murmuring Tibetan mantras. He indicated barely visibly in my direction. His wife came up to me and asked me to follow her. She took my hands, and everything then seemed to happen very quickly. She guided my hands to the hilt of the sword. I saw the blade disappearing into the folds of the dancer's robes, though I could not tell whether and how far it was really sticking into his body. I tried to pull at the sword, but his wife seemed to be telling me to pull harder. She came to my help and the two of us finally succeeded in pulling out the metre long piece of metal. I saw that about 15 centimetres from the tip of the blade was covered with a kind of condensed liquid. Was it sweat? It certainly wasn't blood. But it was moist.

The dancer took up the weapon, leapt in the air, and began his last furious dance. I found my way back to my place, and it seemed to me as if the last minute or two had passed like a dream. I had been too excited and surprised to be aware of exactly what had been going on. Had his wife, when she apparently came to my aid, actually been making it harder for me to draw out the sword, giving me the feeling that I had to use all my strength to pull the blade of the sword out of the dancer's belly?

My hosts had no such doubts. The young men didn't ask me whether the sword was really sticking into the dancer's belly. But they did ask me whether it had really been that difficult to pull out the blade, as had been spoken of for generations. Few of them have tried it themselves; the story lives through its tradition.

The spirit slowly left the body of the man, who was sitting exhausted on his throne. The monks calmly put their musical instruments to one side. The ritual was over, and the neighbourhood visitors were going back home. I sat on the kitchen floor with my hosts and the dancer's family, and we ate sticky red rice and hot *ema datshi*. The dancer joined us, now a farmer and paterfamilias again, smiling and a little abashed. We did not speak about what had just happened.

The Visit from the Reincarnated Man

Even holy men can be subject to avarice

He was suddenly standing in our living room. In his hand he held a bamboo stick, and wrapped round his hips was a red and yellow monk's robe. His socks were full of holes and his shoes were falling apart. He held a bundle of paper money in his hand, most of them 100-*ngultrum* notes.

'I am Ngawang Dorji, Rimpoche from Taktshang. I am eighty years old. I live eight hours above Taktshang monastery. Many years of meditation. Wish you long life and good luck. Want to build one statue of Guru Rimpoche. Need money!'

He waved the bundle of notes to emphasise his request. So this was what a rimpoche looked like, an enlightened reincarnation and a great teacher. This small man, with his astonishingly good English, penetrating eyes and less than modest self-confidence had not chosen Upper Motithang by chance. Ministers, queens and, supposedly, rich *chilips* lived in this posh residential area on the southern slopes above Thimphu.

So we wanted to do our bit. As it is, there could barely be 100,000 statues of Guru Rimpoche in Bhutan, so we were happy to give him 20 *ngultrum*. The holy man took it, looked us deep in the eyes and pronounced firmly:

'Hundred!'

I made it clear that I wasn't about to haggle. 'Long life!' he hissed and – after glancing disdainfully at my cheap trousers from Kathmandu, asked, 'Forty?'

I stood firm, though the long life certainly sounded very tempting. The Rimpoche understood: he had hit upon a tightwad.

The next phase in our guest's plan of attack opened with a rather disarming 'I am hungry!' Renee offered him three apples. Ngawang Dorji's body language made it clear that he knew this kind of apple: they looked good, but they tasted of a mixture of smelly feet and worm-eaten flour.

'Would you like some biscuits?'

If looks could kill … !

Our friend Jigme whispered reverentially that she suspected the Rimpoche wanted a proper meal, such as rice with *ema datshi*. Renee hurried to the microwave. In a Bhutanese household rice is always to be had; there were still the remains of some *ema datshi* in the freezer compartment of our temperamental refrigerator. It had been thawed out and refrozen several times. In the meantime, Ngawang Dorji showed me his admittedly decidedly worn-out footwear, and emphatically compared them with the entire gallery of shoes that were lined up in our hallway. I stood firm.

His Holiness, thankfully, now sat down at the table, and started picking, too late, at his *ema datshi*. The enlightened one clearly figured out quite quickly that the chillies had had a tough time on their long way to his plate. He pushed them disapprovingly aside and tasted the rice. It was, admittedly, the cheapest you could buy, and not the fine, imported basmati rice from India, as one would have expected to find in Motithang. It was farmer's rice, not terribly white, and with a sprinkling of a few brown and black grains. But did that really mean he had to leave his plate half-finished, as if offended by it?

After he had come across the foreign-looking packet of Manner Mignon on a short visit to our kitchen, our guest seemed to change his mind and asked reproachfully for some biscuits. They were the last we had. Back in September 2003 they had crossed the oceans of the world in a container; the heat of Africa's coasts hadn't done the pieces of Manner any good. The crushed biscuits had been fused together by their melted chocolate coating. Renee broke a handful of the unappetising remains out of the packet and handed them to the master of meditative privation.

But he wouldn't take the biscuits from the foreign woman's hand. The least one could have offered His Greediness was the whole packet. Finally a ray of enlightenment fell even upon us. Such humility called for a generous gift. What had once been delicious mignons had degenerated into a crumbling mass of coagulated chocolate. It would sweeten the holy man's frugal and solitary life.

'Long life!' we wished him as he continued on his foray through the villas of Motithang.

Electricity Comes Out
of a Socket

*Even in the remote mountain villages
of the Bhutanese Himalayas*

He knew the Zillertal, a valley in the Austrian Tyrol, well. Chhewang Rinzin, general director of the Bhutan Power electricity company, was in raptures. Taken together, the hydroelectric stations of the Zillertal produced roughly 1,000 megawatts – about as much electricity as Tala, the single largest power station in Bhutan, which joined the grid in August 2006. The income from electricity exports alone would increase the state budget by about 10 per cent.

What is more, Bhutan has been able to unlock its hydroelectric potential without building large dams and reservoirs. Running water is diverted from rivers and carried along high-pressure pipes to power stations, which, depending on the amount of water available, can produce electricity 24 hours a day. The tunnel carrying water to the station at Tala is 23 kilometres long and the second largest in the world.

'India buys every kilowatt-hour at the same price. We mustn't do what they've done in the Alps, which is to build accumulators to store electricity which can be sold at higher prices at times of peak use.' The fact is that the booming Indian economy has an insatiable hunger for energy at every time of the day or year. Hydroelectric power from the Himalayas provides only a small, albeit welcome, contribution to the energy needs of the gigantic Indian national economy.

Bhutan's large neighbour to the south uses about 80 per cent of the electricity produced in Bhutan. In winter it's the other way round: Bhutan needs most of its energy to heat Thimphu and other towns. Climate experts fear that if the glaciers in the Himalayas keep shrinking, the winters will be even dryer.

Electricity from hydroelectric power has lastingly catapulted Bhutan from the list of the poorest countries in the world. Today Western donor nations are already thinking of shifting development co-operation onto a new basis, in view of the kingdom's rapidly growing national income. The country will receive fewer donations in the future, in place of which there will be more loans and advice, for Bhutan with its foreseeable income has become a reliable debtor.

Since the 1980s the largest hydroelectric stations have been built in co-operation with India, while smaller ones were begun with Austrian help. In the beginning the Indians and Austrians donated a great deal, but since then they have required Bhutan to pay for about 60 per cent of their services, and loans from India have been paid for with supplies of electricity. 'We estimate a repayment period of fifteen years; then the investments will belong to us,' said Chhewang Rinzin cheerfully. The electricity supplier in the Zillertal was built with loans from the German state of Baden-Württemburg; at the time the repayment period lasted twenty-five years.

With the opening of the large-scale projects at Basochu, Tala and Kurichu in 2005 and 2006, Bhutan has used up only 5 per cent of the estimated development potential in hydroelectric power. By 2020, production will have tripled.

I asked the general director whether he was worried that hydroelectricity might one day no longer be competitive, especially if American support means that India will start producing nuclear power on a large scale.

'There will always be a market for hydroelectric power. Clean, renewable energy will always be welcome; it's a perfect and flexible addition to other forms of energy.' Chhewang seemed optimistic. What worried him more was regional competition in the Himalayas, above all from Nepal, with its enormous untapped capacities. If the situation there were to stabilise and the country open up for development, competition could arise to become India's sole supplier. If prices started falling, it would be very difficult to develop hydroelectric power.

Even if the simplest thing would just be to export all its electricity to India at good prices – four cents per kilowatt-hour – Bhutan has other plans. By 2020, every Bhutanese household should be connected to the electricity network. 'If all goes well we will meet this target earlier, perhaps in 2017,' said Chhewang, giving a good example of the Bhutanese planning ethic. Nevertheless, at on average $2,000 each, the costs of connecting homes in the mountain villages are among the highest in the world. Bhutan Power bears the costs of supplying electricity to its customers' front door irrespective of where they live, a contribution to Gross National Happiness and a means of promoting equality of opportunity among the rural population. Seventy per cent of Bhutanese are still farmers living in villages that are often above 4,000 metres, some of them reachable only by a day's walk on foot.

Because of their remote location, several hundred of these households will probably be supplied by local micro power stations or solar energy; but the electricity manager's ambitious aim, and the King's explicit order, is that most of them be connected to the grid. By the beginning of 2006 75 per cent of all households were already getting their electricity out of a plug socket. No other country in the region is carrying out the electrification of its rural areas with such dedication.

Let's change the scene. Ugyen was candidate for a teaching post in the small village of Chendibji at the foot of the Black Mountains. We'd arrived late and wanted to visit the small monastery, but it was already dusk. 'No problem,' smiled Ugyen, 'we've got light now.' The ancient monastery's altar room was now illuminated by a 100-watt bulb, and we could take our time admiring its paintings, which were commissioned by the Third King after a fire had badly damaged the building. They were painted in the monastery of Kuenga Rapten, and brought to Chendibji to restore the little shrine to its former glory.

Chendibji is so far from any urban centre that connecting it to any national supply simply would not make any economic sense. So a small, 70-kilowatt power station was built. Since winter 2006 the twenty-five or so households now have light, and there is also enough electricity for cooking rice, warming water and listening to the radio. No doubt someone will eventually get hold of a television and a satellite dish. Ugyen was already dreaming of owning a PC, which would put him in touch with the entire world by e-mail and bring his pupils closer to Bill Gates's world of marvels.

The villagers didn't yet have to pay any electricity bills; they were still having a trial period, smiled Ugyen. The price would be the same as in Thimphu and every other part of the country, although the production costs for the small power station would certainly be many times higher than those for the large installations in the south. The fact that Chendibji now has light in the evening is an outcome of the Kyoto Protocol. The E7, a grouping together of Europe's seven largest energy producers, can buy its way out of having to drastically lower its own emissions by financing renewable energy projects in Third World countries. Ugyen knew the global background. The young teacher was proud of the fact that the first project to be funded this way in Bhutan was in his village. 'People here are happy. Many of them wanted to move away, but now they're thinking again, because with light and electricity the quality of life has got suddenly better.'

Although most households in Bhutan only pay the minimum rate of 35 *ngultrum* per month for their electricity, everyone has a meter. It is, explained Chhewang, a psychological measure. Even if demand is low at present, with most households only using four or five light bulbs, he wants everyone to get a sense of the cost of electrical energy.

The household rate is divided up and promotes energy saving practices. For the first eighty kilowatt-hours per month you pay only a symbolic rate of 60 *chetrum* per kilowatt-hour, which then goes up to 1.10 *ngultrum*, while above 200 kilowatt-hours per month users still pay a modest 1.30 *ngultrum*. India pays two *ngultrum*.

Having electricity does make people happier. Life in the villages has become safer. Outside every farmer's house there is at least one bulb burning the whole night long. Two dozen lights mean that small villages can now be seen from a distance at night, meaning that many of those returning home late can find their way more easily. Also, wild animals avoid the light.

Karmal Prashad Sharma is a Lhotsampa, a southern Bhutanese of Nepalese descent. A few years ago he left his native village of Kalamati in the province of Smatshe; the nightly attacks by jungle elephants on their carefully-worked fields had become intolerable. Now he has returned; his neighbours told him that since there has been electricity the elephants haven't come back. They are afraid of the light. And if an elephant were ever to be in the neighbourhood, then it is a lot easier to quickly organise a group of men to scare the troublemaker away with loud cries and burning torches when there is light to see by.

Bomika Sharma, his fourteen-year-old daughter, has a different relationship with the new energy. She spends many hours sitting in front of the television and dreaming of a life in the city.

Reeking of *ara*, and with his mouth full of betel juice, her grandfather said that he had been content with his life and at seventy-three was really ready to die. But then one day the night turned to day. Light at any hour of the day convinced him to wait for the reincarnation of his eldest son who had died. Only then would he consider dying himself.

Gross National Happiness

Bhutan's state philosophy under scrutiny

'**D**o less, eat less, limit your stress, lose some of your acquisitiveness – and be happier!'

This was how, in response to my question, Karma Ura defined his understanding of Gross National Happiness. Though Bhutan's remarkable state philosophy derives from the opposition between 'gross national happiness' and gross national product, on closer inspection it has little to do with the economic term that gave rise to it.

Karma Ura is Bhutan's best-known writer. His historical novel *The Hero with a Thousand Eyes* has become something of a modern national epic. Today he directs the Centre for Bhutan Studies, whose function is to initiate, publicise and collect works on Bhutan at an international level.

In the meantime it has accumulated an archive of dozens of essays and research papers on Gross National Happiness. But how happy do the Bhutanese really feel? One of the statistical findings of the census of 2005 was an apparent confirmation that the nation considers itself happy. Only 3 per cent of the population answered the question about their personal happiness negatively; 97 per cent described themselves as 'happy' or 'very happy'. But even the *Bhutan Times*, Bhutan's new Sunday newspaper, has questioned whether this was actually the case. After all, for decades people have been told that they were living in the only country in the world where Gross National Happiness had been established as the government's highest purpose.

Ross McDonald, a sociologist from New Zealand, has dealt in detail with the question of whether national happiness and individual contentment are at all dependent upon economic circumstances and achievements. His conclusion was that they weren't; by Gross National Happiness the Bhutanese understood something quite different to simply the feeling of having attained a certain standard of living, for Buddhist thinking would never imagine that one could become happy through the ruthless pursuit of personal success and material gain.

The King himself defines the four pillars of the concept of Gross National Happiness as respect for culture and religion, good governance, economic welfare and care for the environment. Thus it is clear that although prosperity is one factor, true happiness consists not in material goods but in a balance of all four components.

Faced with the armada of ridiculously expensive Toyota landcruisers in which Thimphu's upper classes speed around the tiny capital, one might be forgiven for thinking that indifference to material possessions is not a terribly widespread virtue among the country's Buddhist population. It is precisely with the sharp economic upturn in recent years that Bhutanese society has started experiencing more unhappiness, professional jealousy and dissatisfaction.

Karma Ura concisely defines this process as a 'transition from feudalism to bureaucracy', although Bhutan never really had a feudal system in the European sense of the word. Historically the ruling classes were poor; their power was principally based on social hierarchy or religion, and rarely expressed itself through the possession of material wealth or luxuries. 'Lords and slaves ate from the same plates,' is how the writer describes this unique system, in which those with power are better understood as religious leaders and philosophical advisers than feudal lords.

For centuries Bhutan's indigenous elites were of two kinds. On the one hand there were the orders of monks which boys would join at a very young age, irrespective of social background; on the other there was the civil service which also recruited its members in early youth, taking them from their families to be educated separately, while the rest of the population worked the land and remained uneducated. Even though this is no longer the case today, the self-image of Bhutan's official class has been shaped by their historically privileged position in society. Educated and critical citizens, confident enough to demand a good service from their public servants, are extremely hard to find.

The civil service has maintained its privileges to this day. While in former times many Bhutanese aspired to enter the civil service for the sake of the education and secure standard of living it offered (officials were provided with all living necessities by a tax in kind on the peasantry), today it offers other advantages.

Though the salaries are modest, the standard of living is assured. For several years now there has also been a pension scheme, something that is unknown in the private sector. Officials' social standing could scarcely be any better, hours of work are reasonable, there is a five-day week working thirty to thirty-five hours a week, a month's holiday a year, any number of additional days off for urgent family obligations, and relatively high travel pay; it all adds up to an attractive package. A position in the service also gives one the right to tax breaks when buying a car: most of the four-wheel-drive vehicles that tourists rent in Bhutan belong to high-ranking officials who have bought them tax-free. There are also special perks which, depending on one's rank, can mean a driver or an official apartment.

Bhutan's officials reacted with shock when, as part of preparations for the introduction of democracy, they learned they would have to make their financial circumstances open to public scrutiny. King Jigme Singye Wangchuk has himself decreed a strict regime of anti-corruption inspections for the country, for he sees a possible increase in corruption as the most dangerous side-effect of the introduction of political parties and democratically-elected committees. As a result, officials are being required to set standards for transparency with their personal wealth, in case a civil servant on a modest salary ends up accumulating a disproportionate amount of money.

'It won't make any difference,' said my neighbour, because 'we all know they'll just shift the money to their wives or children so they can come out looking clean.'

Are then Bhutan's notion of Gross National Happiness and the noble contemplation of non-material values nothing more than chimeras? Karma Ura sees things differently. It is still the case that in Bhutan people's circles of friends and their network of social contacts are more important to them than striving for material wealth. There is a highly-developed culture of discussing social and political matters among one's own circle of friends.

But Karma Ura also sees fault lines in the system. 'The introduction of television in 1999 changed our way of thinking. Suddenly we were discussing global themes and forgetting our regional and national concerns.' He also considers the new medium responsible for his countrymen's rapidly growing avidity for consumer goods. Not a week goes by without new products arriving on the market, new shops opening or a new advertising campaign being initiated. Anyone who is anyone has already flown to Bangkok to go shopping, for though Indian goods are duty-free, they are considered less chic than imports from Thailand or Singapore.

Watching television was never expressly forbidden before 1999, but nor was it ever really permitted. This was enough to prevent its introduction, for Bhutan's citizens were used to the idea that they should take satisfaction from performing almost all their daily chores. The first generation of Bhutanese to grow up with forty cable television channels, Internet access and multi-media have already reached school age. It requires no great insight to realise that in the decades to come these people will completely transform the country's traditional pace of life. And 35 per cent of all Bhutanese are under thirteen.

Will Gross National Happiness survive this culture shock? King Jigme Singye Wangchuk has done a great deal to protect his political legacy. He himself is the driving power behind the country's democratisation. Much to his subjects' alarm, he has had a constitution drawn up that aims at turning the last absolute monarchy in the world into a constitutional one. According to the provisions of this document, the monarch must retire when he reaches the age of sixty-five. Although many Bhutanese have urged the King, either personally or in letters to the newspapers, to remove at least this appalling article from the text, the *Druk Gyalpo* surprised his subjects by announcing that he intended to pass the raven crown on to his eldest son as early as 2008.

Bhutan was to have established these new political structures and adopted its modern, democratic constitution on the hundredth anniversary of the founding of the monarchy. However, the celebrations to commemorate the coronation of Sir Ugyen Wangchuk as the first king of Bhutan on 17 December 1907 were not planned to take place until 2008, because astrologers have identified the anniversary year of 2007 as a *lona* or unlucky year. Nothing important should be undertaken in such a year; it is a bad idea to build a house, open a business, marry – or decree a new constitution.

In 2008 King Jigme Singye became, despite his early abdication, one of the longest-serving monarchs in the world, having ascended the throne as a seventeen-year-old following the sudden death of his father in 1972. In Bhutan he is widely regarded as an extremely beloved, modest, and benevolent monarch, and his character considered beyond criticism. Again, it is he himself who sees his people's unquestionable affection in perspective. It seems that many people become decidedly reticent when talking to him, and he has criticised the fact that no one wants to bring him bad news.

He is famed for his unannounced visits to districts and rural communities, which he makes in order to ensure that the places he visits aren't cleaned or tidied up in advance in order to make a good impression. Crown Prince Jigme Khesar Namgyal is already following this example. 'He loves the poor people more than the rich,' is how my friend Taschi describes the future monarch. Neither the King nor his son have anything to do with extravagant foreign visits, expensive lifestyles or regular appearances in the newspaper's gossip columns. On the contrary, both are known for extensive travels around the country, visits to remote mountain villages reachable only by a strenuous march on foot, and for their military service. His Majesty personally led the military incursion against Indian separatists in December 2003. Members of his units report that when they attacked the jungle camps of the United Liberation Front for Assam, he wore the same uniform and carried the same weapons as any other soldier.

There was enormous national excitement when in 2006 the United States' *Time* magazine put King Jigme Singye Wangchuk on its list of the foremost 100 people who are changing our world today. Placed in the category of 'leaders and revolutionaries', the Dragon King, who was preparing to transfer his absolute power to his people, found himself among illustrious company: Hillary Clinton, Bill Gates and Pope Benedict XVI were also on the list, as well as George Bush and Mahmoud Ahmadinejad.

Gross National Happiness, Bhutan's message to the world, is not only a philosophical aspiration but part of its pragmatic politics. But the country which, according to a 1974 article in *Time* magazine, came closest to the Shangri-La of James Hilton's novel, also has its dark and hidden sides. Part of the Buddhist understanding of Gross National Happiness is that happiness is not to be achieved at the cost of others. The persecution of members of Bhutan's Nepalese minority at the end of the 1980s is barely discussed in public, but the small kingdom is burdened by its legacy.

Difficult as it is to measure the degree of happiness of an entire people, there is one fascinating indication that Bhutan may be an exception. Although thousands of Bhutanese have studied abroad over the last three decades, and although attending courses of further education in Europe, America, Thailand or at least India has become prerequisite to even an average career, there are hardly any Bhutanese emigrants in the West. On the contrary, anyone who knows Bhutanese students studying abroad will tell you that they generally suffer a great deal of homesickness, have fresh chilli, red rice and dried fish sent to them from home at great expense, and immediately head back at the end of their course.

'We have no tradition of emigration,' says Karma Ura. 'Our young people have no experience of getting used to new surroundings and little interest in the culture of their host countries or in discovering new worlds.'

Travelling abroad is seen as a chance to buy the modern equivalent of the composite bow, which can then be flashed about at archery practice at home – and to pick up generous travel grants. But true happiness isn't to be found in foreign countries; that's why virtually all students with scholarships to travel abroad are only to glad to get back to the land of Gross National Happiness.

Outlawing Addictions

Tobacco is forbidden, marijuana plants are torn up –
but the Bhutanese still have their addictions

'Thirteen children suspended from school for a month'; the headline on the front page of the *Kuensel*, then Bhutan's only newspaper, referred to an incident that did not fit into the ideal world of Gross National Happiness. The seventeen-year-olds had been caught trying marijuana. In Bhutan, hemp plants grow everywhere; on roadside ditches, in the front gardens of houses, probably even in schoolyards.

Or rather, they used to. Hemp is supposed to have become a thing of the past, since the district of Thimphu mobilised all its forces to eliminate this seductively addictive natural drug. Pupils, teachers and parents have had to spend whole Saturdays pulling up all the marijuana plants in the city area with rakes and shovels, digging up their roots and throwing them on fires.

These working parties put up colourful placards announcing a drug-free society. Every pupil, both male and female, has turned up, and not to do so would have been considered almost inexcusable given that teachers were overseeing the operation. Parents have also been invited to take part in the heroic undertaking, but the number of them attending is somewhat more limited.

In Bhutan marijuana plants are to be found pretty much everywhere, but there is no tradition here of consuming cannabis as a drug. It is only the present generation of young people, the first with access to television and the Internet, who are starting to rather naively experiment with the stuff.

A letter to the newspaper *Kuensel* has also criticised the city authorities' latest ban: from the autumn, all advertising signs must be removed from business premises, as they are spoiling the appearance of the city. Or more precisely: in the future signs on business premises may only refer to activities that appear on the commercial licence of the enterprise in question. If certain premises are divided among several small shops, then these may advertise their wares only on a single board placed over their entrances, indicating for example Coca-Cola or Wai-Wai Noodle Soup and nothing else. Almost a year later the city authorities even decreed that the lettering on the signs be standardised in certain approved colours and sizes; they had now to be in blue with black borders, and the kind of business it is must be indicated in white letters in both *Dzongkha* and English. Shop owners had three months in which to effect these changes, though they are still allowed to choose between three different sizes. According to a spokesman for the city authorities, this enables the city to give the impression of being clean and well organised.

The author of the letter thought that too much had already been banned in Bhutanese society, and that if every ordinary practice were banned they were running the risk of losing touch with the times. 'You can't ban everything.'

All this had started years ago with the 'ban on plastic'. Environmental concerns prompted the Thimphu city authorities to forbid the use of plastic bags and packaging. People got used to it. Anyone going shopping at the market took baskets or shopping bags with him, since no sellers were allowed to give you plastic bags. It would actually have worked quite well if only, for want of recycling bins, thousands of plastic bottles that had once contained mineral water, Coca-Cola and soda had not ended up being thrown away with all the other trash. As it was, they were carted off twice a week in huge quantities by the city's highly efficient rubbish collection teams.

The ban on selling meat has a religious basis to it. Since Buddhists are not really supposed to kill any living creatures, butchers' shops are considered fundamentally objectionable. The profession of butcher is practised either by Hindu migrants or in the villages by a family that has to some degree been stigmatised, and which generally hands its bloody trade down from father to son. But since the Bhutanese are extremely fond of yak meat, pork and chopped chicken, they forgive these poor sinners their business. Thimphu's city authorities, however, wanted to put a stop to this shameless activity at least on Sundays and religious holidays. Thus the butchers' shops, and the rather shamefully tucked-away stalls selling meat at the weekly markets, remain shut on these 'auspicious days'. The open trade in meat in the first and fourth month of the Buddhist calendar is also completely forbidden.

When we arrived for supper at Jambayang, our favourite Thimphu restaurant, the waiter explained that there were no meat dishes on the menu because of the month of fast. Then he added somewhat conciliatorily that there was in fact some chicken. My companion Uden decided against this. Anyone wanting to avoid the total ban on eating meat that comes in the new year, right after the festival of Lhosar, can do this if he or she eats absolutely no fish, chicken or eggs during this time. If you observe this rule, then you can safely give in to your longings for dried yak meat or pork crackling. But in no circumstances should one eat eggs during this important month, for one never knows whether a small embryo might have been growing inside the egg. This is frequently the case with local farmers' eggs; with cheaper eggs imported from large batteries in India the danger is not so great. Uden knew that 'eating an egg with an embryo is worse than killing 500 monks'. We decided not to take any risks and ordered vegetarian dishes.

In this journey towards an addiction-free and healthy society, the ban on alcohol was, from the beginning, only ever half-heartedly put into practice. The Bhutanese are far too fond of the products of the 'Army Welfare Project', a distillery that belongs to the Royal Bhutan Army and whose profits supply pension funds for its members. Black Mountain Whisky costs less than 2 euros a bottle, while the top-quality Special Courier, in its red and gold luxury presentation box, costs just over 3. In addition to these there is a huge quantity of cheap, rough liquors, including home-made *ara* distilled from rice, wheat or millet, which is particularly plentiful in the countryside. Nevertheless, in Thimphu there is a 'dry day'. On Tuesdays the sale of alcoholic drinks in the city's bars and pubs is forbidden, and most of them shut on this day since it isn't worth staying open.

Ambivalence towards the Demon Drink is particularly striking. Every opportunity is used to warn people of the dangers of alcohol abuse; posters hang in health centres, and reports in the *Kuensel* deal with the drug's negative effects on individuals and society. On the next page, however, you are likely to find a full-page insert by the Army Welfare Project announcing the official sale prices of its most popular spirits. It has come to their attention that whisky, gin and brandy are being sold in many places at inflated prices, the text explains; their customers are hereby informed of the actual prices of their goods, so that they do not find themselves paying over the odds.

But perhaps the ban that has received most publicity abroad is the one on the sale of tobacco products, which began at the start of 2005. The 'smoking ban' has without doubt been the most widely reported of news stories from the hidden kingdom. But reports that the government has forbidden smoking everywhere in the country have been somewhat less than accurate.

For smoking itself is not forbidden; it is the trade in tobacco that is. There are no tobacco plantations or cigarette factories in Bhutan, so all smoking products must be imported. This is where the ban comes into force. Even tourists may from now on only bring a maximum of 200 cigarettes into the country with them, on each of which they must pay a 200 per cent import duty; when packets have already been opened, every cigarette is counted. Most of those caught end up giving all their cigarettes to customs officers to be destroyed, and receive in return a written confirmation of this.

Nevertheless, the black market is booming, even though every edition of the *Kuensel* reports the truly draconian punishments being meted out to smugglers. A 20,000-*ngultrum* fine for a taxi driver who had eighteen packets of cheap Indian cigarettes under his passenger seat; prison for a market trader who could not pay the 9,000-*ngultrum* fine she had incurred for selling tobacco. In the meantime, the price of under-the-counter cigarettes has risen so high that many Bhutanese can barely afford to indulge their addiction.

Smoking in public buildings, offices, restaurants and bars is forbidden. But every official knows of a room in his building where chain-smokers bravely defy the smoking ban, naturally behind closed doors; occasionally half the department joins their smoking colleague for a 'business meeting'. Of course, addicts know exactly which bars and pubs have at least a back room where you can smoke.

Yet for all this, this ban has produced a lasting change in Bhutanese society. For some time now even those who break the ban out of conviction have no longer been bragging about it. Those who talked knowingly of the failure of Prohibition in the United States during the 1920s have grown noticeably quieter. Lighting-up has simply become unchic, unless it is among a close circle of like-minded friends; people have started apologising for lighting up or even feeling embarrassed.

There is no ban on the popular narcotic *doma*, however. There is no doubt that chewing the areca nut, covered with a layer of dried chalk and wrapped in betel tree leaves, is the kingdom's number one drug problem. The areca nut grows on a palm that is cultivated in the large plantations in southern Bhutan. Hundreds of thousands of Bhutanese are addicted to it, chewing *doma* anything between five to fifty times a day and spitting its reddish brown remains into literally every corner of the realm. The drug causes them to progressively lose their (by then) deeply red-stained teeth, because, while the chewing prevents tooth decay, it leads to progressive gum recession; it also causes stomach ulcers and gastritis.

Despite this, *doma* does not have any intoxicating or even mind-altering effects. Wrapped in betel leaves, the nut is put carefully in the mouth in order to ensure that the chalk does not come in contact with the inside of the mouth, which would lead to severe burns. The strange mixture is sucked for minutes on end, all the time moved from one cheek into the other. Only then does one begin carefully biting into the initially rock-hard nut, which slowly crumbles into dozens of jagged pieces.

This causes users to salivate a great deal, and minutes later the heart rate increases and they feel a warm shiver that brings their foreheads out in a sweat. This warm feeling can be particularly pleasant during the cold months of the year, but the effect wears off in five or ten minutes, and all that remains is a slight tiredness and a red, evil-smelling pulp in the mouth. It is swallowing this that can lead to stomach ulcers and gastritis, so it is usually spat out – in every conceivable, and inconceivable, place.

Any visitor crossing an old cantilever bridge might imagine himself to be on the site of some savage battle if he mistakes the red stains lying around for blood. Originally *doma* was spat out everywhere, and white-washed walls in ministries, museums and market halls are accordingly coloured red. Today the authorities are attempting to limit the spitting to certain designated areas, a process which is likely to take at least a generation or two to succeed.

In contrast to other drugs, *doma* is not socially disapproved of. Polite, reserved and humble officials will appear before their superiors at official meetings, shove the small green packets into their mouths during the meeting as if it were the most natural thing in the world, become temporarily distracted as the mixture of spit and nut remains overflows in his mouth, wipes the sweat off his brow once the effect kicks in and leaves the conference room to deposit the red, putrid end-product.

Doma observes no social barriers, and the drug costs only a few cents. It is considered good form for people to offer each other *doma* at every meeting. Even participants in religious ceremonies are given betel leaves and areca nut as part of the ritual. Sophisticated users are also aware that the unseemly reddening of the teeth can be avoided by brushing them after use, and Western visitors find the sight of red teeth easier to bear than the penetrating stench spread by the drug.

However, no one has attempted to ban the chewing of *doma*. 'That would be political suicide,' reflected one high-ranking official – rather as if Angela Merkel were to restrict the speed limit on German motorways to 70 miles per hour.

Glossary

Ara – local schnapps.

Ashi – Queen.

Chilip – foreigner.

Chorten – religious monument made of stone which sometimes contains relics. Frequently built in holy places in memory of someone who has died.

Chugo – smoked yak cheese.

Chyang – slightly alcoholic drink brewed from grapes.

Dasho – Bhutanese title, roughly equivalent to a knighthood.

Doma – the country's national drug: areca nut, betel leaves and chalk paste.

Druk – Thunder Dragon.

Druk Gyalpo – the king's official title in Bhutan.

Drukpa – People of the Thunder Dragon; the group of Tibetan people who at the beginning of the 6th century migrated from Tibet to Bhutan under the leadership of the first Shabdrung of Tibet.

Druk Yul – Land of the Thunder Dragon (Bhutan's official name).

Drungtso – traditional doctor.

Dzong – monastery town, seat of the local administration and the most important monastery in the district (earlier a defensive complex).

Dzongkha – the national language (literally 'the language they speak in Dzong').

Dzongpen – prince of a region.

Ema datshi – chilli with cheese sauce.

Gho – men's traditional costume: a skirt tied about the hips with a belt.

Guru Rimpoche – National saint, visited Bhutan in the 8th century, father of Mahayana Buddhism, reincarnation of the historical Buddha.

Kaddar – ceremonial veil; traditional good-luck gift.

Kira – women's national dress: wrap-around skirt made from hand-woven material.

Lam – high monk, abbot; *lama* – monk.

Lhakhang – monastery.

Mangap – village headman.

Ngultrum – Bhutan's currency; 1 *ngultrum* = 100 *chetrum*. At the time of writing, there were approximately 50 *ngultrum* to the Euro.

Penlop – sovereign prince.

Puja – religious ceremony.

Shabdrung – title of the reincarnated spiritual and temporal leader of the *Drukpa*.

Suja – salted butter tea.

Thanka – Buddhist scroll with religious motifs.

Tsachu – hot springs (literally: hot water).

Tsechu – monastic festival involving a masked dance, usually lasting three days.